John Wilson 2002
UBC science FIrst year

Crystallization-Study
of
Philippians

Volume Two

The Holy Word for Morning Revival

Witness Lee

Living Stream Ministry
Anaheim, California

First Edition, August 2002.

ISBN 0-7363-1879-8

Published by

Living Stream Ministry
2431 W. La Palma Ave., Anaheim, CA 92801 U.S.A.
P. O. Box 2121, Anaheim, CA 92814 U.S.A.

Printed in the United States of America

02 03 04 05 06 07 08 / 10 9 8 7 6 5 4 3 2 1

Contents

iii

Preface

1. This book is intended as an aid to believers in developing a daily time of morning revival with the Lord in His word. At the same time, it provides a review of the 2002 Summer Training on the "Crystallization-study of Philippians." Through intimate contact with the Lord in His word, the believers can be constituted with life and truth and thereby equipped to prophesy in the meetings of the church unto the building up of the Body of Christ.

2. The content of this book is taken primarily from the *Crystallization-study Outlines,* the text and footnotes of the Recovery Version of the Bible, selections from the writings of Watchman Nee and Witness Lee, and *Hymns,* all of which are published by Living Stream Ministry.

3. The book is divided into weeks. One training message is covered per week. Each week first presents the message outline, followed by six daily portions, a hymn, and then some space for writing. The message outline has been divided into days, corresponding to the six daily portions. Each daily portion covers certain points and begins with a section entitled "Morning Nourishment." This section contains selected verses and a short reading that can provide rich spiritual nourishment through intimate fellowship with the Lord. The "Morning Nourishment" is followed by a section entitled "Today's Reading," a longer portion of ministry related to the day's main points. Each day's portion concludes with a short list of references for further reading and some space for the saints to make notes concerning their spiritual inspiration, enlightenment, and enjoyment to serve as a reminder of what they have received of the Lord that day.

4. The space provided at the end of each week is for composing a short prophecy. This prophecy can be composed by considering all our daily notes, the "harvest" of our inspirations during the week, and preparing a main point with some sub-points to be spoken in the church meetings for the organic building up of the Body of Christ.

5. The *Crystallization-study Outlines* were compiled by Living Stream Ministry from the writings of Watchman Nee and Witness Lee. The outlines, footnotes, and references in the Recovery Version of the Bible were written by Witness Lee. All of the other references cited in this publication are from the ministry of Watchman Nee and Witness Lee.

2002 Summer Training

CRYSTALLIZATION-STUDY
OF PHILIPPIANS

Banners:

**The Christian life is a life of living Christ
for the constitution and building up
of the Body of Christ.**

**We need to work out our own salvation
by obeying the inner operating God.**

**We need to be conformed
to the mold of Christ's death
by the power of His resurrection
that we may attain to the out-resurrection
from the dead.**

**The Christian life is a life full of Christ
as forbearance but without anxiety.**

Taking Christ as Our Goal (1)
Counting All Things to Be Loss on account of the Excellency of the Knowledge of Christ

Scripture Reading: Phil. 3:4-14

Day 1

I. **Chapter three of Philippians shows us that Christ must be our goal and our aim (vv. 12-14):**
   A. For Christ to be the goal means that He is the highest enjoyment.
   B. Our goal is the all-inclusive Christ as the prize to be awarded to us; when we reach the goal, the goal will immediately become the prize (v. 14).
   C. Paul's pursuit was toward one goal, one aim— Christ; he took Christ as his goal, pursuing to obtain the prize to which God in Christ Jesus had called him upward.
   D. Since our goal is to gain Christ, we should forsake all other things and pursue nothing but Christ (vv. 7-8, 12-14).

Day 2

II. **Saul of Tarsus had a vision of the Lord Jesus; this vision gave him the excellency of the knowledge of Christ (Acts 9:1-5; 22:6-11; 26:13-16; Gal. 1:15a, 16a; Phil. 3:8):**
   A. It is important for us to realize that in Philippians 3:8 Paul does not speak directly of the excellency of Christ but speaks of the excellency of the knowledge of Christ:
      1. This knowledge is not the knowledge that belongs to Christ, the knowledge that Christ Himself has; it is our subjective knowing of Christ.
      2. In verse 8 *knowledge* actually means a revelation, a vision, concerning Christ and His excellence.

Day 3

   B. The excellency of the knowledge of Christ is derived from the excellency of His person (Matt. 17:5; Col. 1:13):
      1. The entire Bible is a revelation of the wonderful

person of Christ; how excellent and inexhaustible He is!

2. When Christ was revealed to Paul, he saw that the excellency, the super-eminence, the supreme preciousness, the surpassing worth, of Christ far exceeded the excellency of the law (Gal. 1:15a, 16a).

3. The excellency of the knowledge of Christ is the excellency of Christ realized by us.

4. If we lack the knowledge of Christ's excellency, His excellency will not mean anything to us.

5. Christ is unlimited; we need to have the excellency of the knowledge of the unlimited Christ (Col. 1:12, 15-19; 2:2-3, 9, 16-17; 3:10).

6. We need to have a vision of the preciousness of Christ (1 Pet. 2:4, 7).

C. The excellency of the knowledge of Christ comes by revelation (Matt. 16:17):

1. Without the revelation concerning Christ, we would not know Christ; revelation is for knowing (11:27; Gal. 1:15a, 16a).

2. We need to see a vision and receive a revelation of the excellency of Christ; if we have a revelation of Christ's excellency, we shall automatically have the excellency of the knowledge of Christ.

Day 4 D. In order to experience Christ, we first need to have the excellency of the knowledge of Christ (Phil. 3:7-10):

1. To know Christ is crucial to our experience of Him; we cannot experience Him without knowing Him (Gal. 1:15a, 16a; 2:20; 4:19).

2. Our experience of Christ cannot surpass the excellency of our knowledge of Christ (Eph. 1:17-21; 3:14-19):

a. The excellency of the knowledge of Christ always exceeds our experience of Christ.

b. There has never been a believer whose experience of Christ surpassed his knowledge of Christ.

c. If we do not have a higher knowledge of Christ, we cannot have a higher experience of Christ.

Day 5 III. **On account of the excellency of the knowledge of Christ, Paul counted all things to be loss, and he suffered the loss of all things, counting them as refuse that he might gain Christ (Phil. 3:7-8):**

A. Paul's eyes were opened to see the excellency of the knowledge of the wonderful, all-inclusive Christ; on account of this excellency, he counted as loss all things, whether they related to religious gain or natural gain:

1. All things which were once gains to Paul hindered him and held him back from participating in Christ and enjoying Him:

a. In verse 7 *what things* refers to the religious things, the things in Judaism; Paul dropped all those religious things for Christ (vv. 4-6).

b. In verse 8 *all things* indicates that Paul dropped not only religious things but all things on account of the excellency of the knowledge of Christ Jesus; thus, to Paul, the loss of all things was the loss not only of his Jewish status but of everything.

2. Paul placed great value upon the excellency of the knowledge of his dear Lord Jesus Christ (vv. 7-8).

3. For the excellency of the knowledge of Christ, which he treasured, Paul counted everything as refuse, dregs, rubbish, filth, that which is thrown to the dogs (v. 8).

Day 6 B. The way for us to experience Christ and enjoy Christ is to deny everything we have and are (vv. 4-6, 13b):

1. The greatest obstacle to enjoying Christ is our natural heritage:
   a. Nothing natural should be allowed to replace Christ.
   b. Any naturally good thing will frustrate us from the enjoyment of Christ (1 Cor. 2:14).
2. The way to enjoy Christ is to reject everything that we are by nature; everything must go, and only Christ must remain (1:26-30; 2:1-2).
3. If we have more of the excellency of the knowledge of Christ, we will drop everything religious and everything natural on account of Him and on account of the excellency of the knowledge of Him (Phil. 3:7-8).

Morning Nourishment

**Phil. Not that I have already obtained or am already
3:12-14 perfected, but I pursue, if even I may lay hold of
that for which I also have been laid hold of by
Christ Jesus. Brothers, I do not account of myself
to have laid hold; but one thing *I do:* Forgetting
the things which are behind and stretching forward to the things which are before, I pursue
toward the goal for the prize to which God in
Christ Jesus has called *me* upward.**

Chapter three of Philippians shows us that Christ must be
our goal and our aim. Verse 14 speaks of the goal. We are in a
race, and our goal is the all-inclusive Christ. When the apostle
Paul wrote this Epistle in approximately A.D. 64, he was already quite old and had been running the Christian race for a
long time. Although Paul was aged and very experienced in
Christ, he did not have the assurance that he had arrived at
the goal. He was even afraid that he would miss the mark. So
he said, "Forgetting the things which are behind and stretching
forward to the things which are before, I pursue toward the
goal" (vv. 13b-14a). The goal is Christ Himself as the prize to
be awarded to us. In the Old Testament the good land of
Canaan was the goal for all the people of Israel after they were
saved and delivered out of Egypt. While they were wandering
and pressing on in the wilderness, they had a goal ahead of
them. The good land of Canaan is a type of Christ, who is our
goal. (*A General Sketch of the New Testament in the Light of
Christ and the Church,* pp. 215-216)

Today's Reading

Paul undoubtedly was of a very strong character, both when
he was Saul of Tarsus and when he was Paul the apostle. Being
of a strong character, he never did anything halfway. When he
was Saul of Tarsus, he persecuted the church negatively, and after
he became the apostle Paul, he persecuted Christ positively.

In order to experience Christ, in this sense we need to

persecute Him. When some hear such a word, they may say, "It is heresy to say that we, the lovers of Christ, should persecute Him." Yes, we need to persecute Christ....When this is viewed in a positive sense, it is not too much of an extreme. Mary Magdalene was an example of one who persecuted the Lord Jesus in a positive way. Early in the morning on the day of His resurrection, she pursued Him. She persecuted the resurrected Christ and persuaded Him to do something that He was not willing to do. We all need to seek the Lord in such a way.

Both the goal and the prize are Christ. Christ is within us, but He is also before us at the end of the race as the goal that we are striving to reach. To say that Christ is the goal means that He is the highest enjoyment. The Christ who is in us for our enjoyment today is not the goal. The goal is the highest enjoyment of Christ, that is, the out-resurrection. No matter how much we experience Christ today, we have not yet reached the goal of the highest enjoyment of Christ. This experience of Christ is still before us. As soon as we reach the goal, the goal will immediately become the prize. When you obtain the prize, you may shout with the enjoyment of the highest experience of Christ. At that time, you will have the out-resurrection as the top enjoyment. Therefore, the enjoyment is Christ, the experience is Christ, the goal is Christ, and the prize is Christ. Christ is the enjoyment within us, and Christ is the goal set before us. We need to pursue toward the goal so that we may gain the prize.

To pursue Christ in this way we need to be aggressive and to exercise ourselves very much. No lazy person can be a persecutor of Christ. Every persecutor of Christ has a strong character. I say again that we all must pursue Christ in a persecuting way. We need to pray,...telling the Lord that we shall persecute Him until He becomes our experience. If we do this, eventually we shall arrive at the goal and receive the prize. (*The Experience of Christ,* pp. 181-183)

Further Reading: A General Sketch of the New Testament in the Light of Christ and the Church, ch. 18; *The Experience of Christ,* ch. 20; *Life-study of Philippians,* msg. 23

Enlightenment and inspiration: _____
_____

Morning Nourishment

Phil. But moreover I also count all things to be loss on
3:8 account of the excellency of the knowledge of
Christ Jesus my Lord, on account of whom I have
suffered the loss of all things and count *them* as
refuse that I may gain Christ.

Gal. But when it pleased God, who set me apart from
1:15-16 my mother's womb and called me through His
grace, to reveal His Son in me that I might announce Him as the gospel among the Gentiles,
immediately I did not confer with flesh and blood.

It is important to realize that in Philippians 3:8 Paul does
not speak of the excellency of Christ but of the excellency of
the knowledge of Christ. Many readers of Philippians take the
word *excellency* to refer not to the knowledge of Christ but to
Christ Himself. However, Paul specifically and definitely
speaks of the excellency of the knowledge of Christ. Paul's
knowledge of Christ was excellent. On account of the excellency
of this knowledge, he was willing to suffer the loss of all things.

In verse 7 Paul says "on account of Christ," but in verse 8
he goes further and says "on account of the excellency of the
knowledge of Christ Jesus my Lord." The addition of the words
my Lord indicates that as Paul was writing, he was filled with
intimate, tender feelings concerning Christ. Tender feelings
concerning the preciousness of the Lord Jesus rose up within
him, causing him to speak of "Christ Jesus my Lord." Paul
placed great value on the excellency of the knowledge of his
dear Lord Jesus Christ. (*Life-study of Philippians,* pp. 156-157)

Today's Reading

The excellency of the knowledge of Christ is derived from the
excellency of His person. The Jews consider the law of God given
through Moses the most excellent thing in history. Hence, they
are zealous for the law. Paul participated in that zeal. But when
Christ was revealed to him by God (Gal. 1:15-16), he saw that
the excellency, the supereminence, the supreme preciousness,

the surpassing worth, of Christ far exceeded the excellency of the law. His knowledge of Christ issued in the excellency of the knowledge of Christ. On account of this, not only did he account the law and the religion founded on the law to be loss, but he counted all things loss.

Here Paul speaks not directly of the excellency of Christ but of the excellency of knowing Christ. The knowledge in 3:8 is not the knowledge that belongs to Christ, the knowledge that Christ Himself has; it is our subjective knowing of Christ. To you, which is more excellent—the person of Christ or your knowing Christ? According to doctrine or opinion, you may say that the person of Christ is more excellent than the knowledge of Christ. However, Paul, speaking from his experience, could say that it is the knowledge of Christ which is more excellent.

Before Paul's experience on the road to Damascus, he did not have any knowledge of Christ. He treasured the law and regarded it as most excellent. Paul's zeal for the law was a sign of his appreciation of the law. His zeal came out of his appreciation. Paul certainly was proud of his excellent knowledge of the law. Even though Christ is infinitely more excellent than the law, Paul did not have the knowledge of Christ. But at the time of his conversion, this excellent One was revealed to him. With this revelation of Christ, Paul began to have the knowledge of Christ...[and] came to realize that the knowledge of the law... was far inferior to the knowledge of Christ. Conscious of this comparison as he was writing 3:5-8, Paul could speak of the excellency of the knowledge of Christ and of suffering the loss of all things for the excellency of this knowledge.

To be sure, the excellency is in the very person of Christ. But for our experience, our realization of this excellency depends on our knowledge. If we lack knowledge, there is simply no way for us to realize that this Person is so excellent. Only when we come to know His excellency do we have the excellency of the knowledge of Christ. How precious is this excellency of the knowledge of Christ! (*Life-study of Philippians,* pp. 157-158)

Further Reading: Life-study of Philippians, msg. 19

__Enlightenment and inspiration:__ _____

_____

Morning Nourishment

Col. And He is before all things, and all things cohere in
1:17-19 Him; and He is the Head of the Body, the church; He
is the beginning, the Firstborn from the dead, that
He Himself might have the first place in all things;
for in Him all the fullness was pleased to dwell.

The merchants [in Hong Kong] know how to display their
products, especially jade, in a way to make them very attractive
to tourists. Often when tourists see precious items on display,
they become excited. Furthermore, they acquire a knowledge
of the excellency of these things. Before they entered the store,
they did not know anything of the excellency of these precious
items. But once they saw them and gained the excellency of
the knowledge concerning them, they were willing to pay the
price to possess them. In like manner, we need a revelation of
Christ's excellency, of His supreme preciousness.

My burden in this message is not related to doctrine...[but]
that we see a vision and receive a revelation of the excellency
of Christ. If we have a revelation of Christ's excellency, we shall
automatically have the excellency of the knowledge of Christ.

The excellency of the knowledge of Christ is in Philippians
3:8, whereas the actual experience of Christ is in 3:10. The
knowledge of Christ, however, is basic. By knowledge we actually mean a revelation, a vision, concerning Christ and His
excellence. When Paul was blind and in religion, he could not
see Christ; he could see only the law. Thus, he had the excellency
of the knowledge of the law. But after Christ was revealed to
him, he began to have the excellency of the knowledge of Christ.
He was captured by the excellency of knowing Christ, and for
the sake of this knowledge, he was willing to drop all things and
count them to be loss. (*Life-study of Philippians,* pp. 161-162)

Today's Reading

We need to be impressed with the all-inclusiveness of Christ.
The Gospel of John reveals that Christ is God, that He is the
Creator, that in Him is life, and that this life is the light of men

(John 1:1-4). One day, He, the Word, became flesh, full of grace and truth (v. 14). According to Colossians, Christ is the image of the invisible God, the Firstborn of every creature, and the One in whom all things were made and in whom they consist (Col. 1:15-17). Christ holds together in Himself the entire universe. Hebrews 1:3 says that He upholds all things by the word of His power. For example, the planet earth is neither too close to the sun nor too far from it. If the earth were too close, it would be burned, and if it were too far, it would be frozen. The Lord Jesus Christ is the One responsible for keeping the earth in its proper position in relation to the sun. The very Christ who does this is also our life. If He can regulate the earth and the sun, then He can certainly regulate us, and He can surely regulate our relationship with our husband or wife. The Christ who upholds the universe and in whom all things consist upholds the relationship between a husband and his wife. The reason so many marriages end in divorce is that in those marriages there are two spokes without a hub. Hallelujah, we have the all-inclusive Christ as our hub!

Colossians 1:18 goes on to say that Christ is the Firstborn from the dead. Hence, He is not only the Firstborn in creation, but also the Firstborn in resurrection. Both in the old creation and in the new creation, He is the Firstborn. Therefore, He is the Head of the church. Colossians also reveals that it pleased the Father that all His fullness would be embodied in Christ (1:19).

Many who talk about Christ speak of Him in a light, superficial way. Christ is unlimited. We need to have the excellency of the knowledge of this unlimited Christ, who is our Lord. On account of this Person, Christ Jesus the Lord, the apostle Paul suffered the loss of all things. This was the cause. The effect issuing from this cause was that Paul gained Christ. On account of Christ, he suffered the loss of all things in order that he might gain Christ. (*The Experience of Christ*, pp. 111-112)

Further Reading: Life-study of Philippians, msgs. 19-20; The Experience of Christ, ch. 13

Enlightenment and inspiration: _____

_____

_____

_____

Morning Nourishment

Eph. That the God of our Lord Jesus Christ, the Father of
1:17-18 glory, may give to you a spirit of wisdom and revelation in the full knowledge of Him, the eyes of your
heart having been enlightened, that you may know
what is the hope of His calling, and what are the
riches of the glory of His inheritance in the saints.
Phil. To know Him and the power of His resurrection
3:10-11 and the fellowship of His sufferings, being conformed to His death, if perhaps I may attain to the
out-resurrection from the dead.

There has never been a case where a believer's experience
of Christ surpassed his knowledge of Christ. If we do not have
a higher knowledge of Christ, we cannot have a higher experience of Christ. This is why it is very important that we not be
limited by our past knowledge of Christ.

You may know that Christ is joy, peace, and rest. Before you
were saved, you did not have the peace. But now that you have
received the Lord, you have peace and joy....Nevertheless, we
should not be content with such a limited knowledge of Christ,
but should advance in our knowledge of Him. Oh, how we need
the excellency of knowing Christ!

The excellency of the knowledge of Christ will attract us to
Christ and motivate us to lay aside everything other than Him.
If we see the surpassing worth of Christ, we shall be willing to
count as loss not only worldly, material things, but even our
culture, religion, and philosophy. I repeat, it is the excellency
of the knowledge of Christ which causes us to drop everything
else so that we may gain Christ and be found in Him. (*Life-
study of Philippians*, p. 173)

Today's Reading

In Philippians 3:7 through 11 Paul brings us higher and
higher. These verses are...like ascending steps of a staircase.

Each verse brings us higher and higher until we reach the peak in verse 11....We should not be content with simply an elementary knowledge of spiritual things. We need to learn what is the excellency of the knowledge of Christ and what it means to count all things to be refuse; what it is to gain Christ and be found in Him; what it is to know Him, the power of His resurrection, and the fellowship of His sufferings. We also need to grasp what it means to be conformed to the death of Christ....Because these matters are deep, we cannot understand them quickly or easily.

We should not be satisfied to remain superficial Christians. The book of Philippians is not an elementary writing; it is a book in the "graduate school" of spiritual experience. Thus, we should not be content merely with a general knowledge of this book. On the contrary, we need to become familiar with the extraordinary expressions Paul uses in this Epistle. Before we can have the experience, we must become familiar with Paul's expressions. This will bring us out of our oldness and save us from being so common and general in speaking of Christ. May the Lord grant us mercy that we may have more knowledge of Christ in order to have more experience of Him.

Even though we may love the Lord very much and daily take time to pray ourselves into the Spirit, in our actual living we may live in things other than Christ. The Chinese saints may live in their ethics, and the British saints may live in their diplomacy. We live this way automatically and spontaneously. How we need a vision of the excellency of Christ. If we have the excellency of the knowledge of Christ, we shall see that He far surpasses the best national characteristics. We shall know that Christ is far superior to every element of our culture. Only the excellency of the knowledge of Christ will rid us of the influence of all the things that are not Christ Himself. (*Life-study of Philippians*, pp. 177-178, 181-182)

Further Reading: Life-study of Philippians, msgs. 20-22

Enlightenment and inspiration: _____

_____

_____

_____

Morning Nourishment

Phil. **Circumcised the eighth day; of the race of Israel,**
3:5-8 **of the tribe of Benjamin, a Hebrew *born* of He-**
brews; as to the law, a Pharisee; as to zeal, perse-
cuting the church; as to the righteousness which
is in the law, become blameless. But what things
were gains to me, these I have counted as loss on
account of Christ. But moreover I also count all
things to be loss on account of the excellency of
the knowledge of Christ Jesus my Lord, on ac-
count of whom I have suffered the loss of all things
and count *them* as refuse that I may gain Christ.

Before his experience on the road to Damascus, Paul did not
have the excellency of the knowledge of Christ. He treasured
the law and was zealous and righteous according to the law.
But one day his eyes were opened to see the excellency of the
knowledge of the wonderful One. On account of this excellency,
he counted as loss all things, whether they were related to
religious gain or natural gain. Paul said that he counted all
things loss for the excellency of the knowledge of Christ Jesus
the Lord. *Christ* refers to God's anointed and appointed One,
the Messiah, who accomplishes everything God has purposed.
Jesus is the name of the Nazarene who lived in Palestine. Today
Jesus Christ is *our* Lord. This means that He has something
to do with us. On account of the excellency of the knowledge of
this wonderful One, we count all things loss. Furthermore, we
even suffer the loss of all things. I would like to cast everything
aside on account of this Person. Compared to Him, all other
things are dung, dog food. When Paul was one of the "dogs" in
Judaism, he needed dog food. But when he became a son of the
living God, he had no further need for it....We are no longer
dogs feeding on refuse; we are sons of God feeding on Christ
Jesus our Lord. (*The Experience of Christ*, pp. 109-110)

Today's Reading

Philippians 3:8 speaks of the excellency of the knowledge

of Christ. Paul does not say "the excellency of Christ," but "the excellency of the knowledge of Christ." To experience Christ we firstly need the knowledge of Christ. We must know Him. This chapter stresses very much the knowledge of Christ. Verse 10 says, "To know Him and the power of His resurrection." Therefore to know Him is crucial to our experience of Him. We cannot experience Him without knowing Him. The knowledge of Christ is excellent, and this knowledge is even an excellency. Paul counted everything refuse, rubbish, dog food, for the excellency of knowing Christ. Most readers of Philippians 3 consider the excellency here to be the excellency of Christ the person. However, this is not correct. We must stress here the knowing of Christ. Christ Himself stressed that He would build His church not upon Himself as the rock but upon the revelation concerning Him. The revelation is for knowing. Without the revelation concerning Christ surely we could not know Him. We need this revelation to know Christ. When Paul was Saul of Tarsus, Christ was there, having passed through all the major steps, perfected, completed, and consummated in full. However, Saul of Tarsus had no knowledge concerning this Christ. On his way to Damascus the day dawned and the light came. He began to see the vision, the revelation concerning Christ (Acts 26:19). By seeing this vision he gained a knowledge, and that knowledge became to him a treasure, an excellency. For this knowledge, which he treasured, he counted everything as refuse, dregs, rubbish, filth, which is thrown to the dogs, the dog food or dung.

Among all the things which Paul counted dung, the first was the religious or Judaic things. In verses 5 and 6 he gives us a list of his Judaic status. He counted not only these things as loss but also all things, including rank, position, fame, and wealth. The loss of all things to Paul was the loss not only of his Jewish status but of everything. (*Elders' Training, Book 6: The Crucial Points of the Truth in Paul's Epistles*, pp. 91-92)

Further Reading: The Experience of Christ, ch. 12; *Elders' Training, Book 6: The Crucial Points of the Truth in Paul's Epistles*, ch. 7; *Life-study of Philippians*, msgs. 18, 21

Enlightenment and inspiration: _____

_____

Morning Nourishment

Phil. 3:13 ...One thing *I do:* Forgetting the things which are behind and stretching forward to the things which are before.

1 Cor. 2:1-2 And I, when I came to you, brothers, came not according to excellence of speech or of wisdom, announcing to you the mystery of God. For I did not determine to know anything among you except Jesus Christ, and this One crucified.

The way for us to enjoy Christ is to deny everything we have and are. We must even deny the best spiritual experiences we have had. The way to eat Christ is to deny everything and to come to Him empty-handed. If you empty out your whole being, He will be something new to you.

Paul not only counted all things loss for the sake of Christ, but counted all things as dung. According to his accounting, everything meant nothing. Because he always counted everything loss for the sake of Christ, he constantly enjoyed Christ. The more things you deny, the more Christ will replace you and the more He becomes your experience and enjoyment. Our slogan should be this: "Oh, that I may gain Christ!" Oh, that we may also obtain that for which we have been obtained by Christ. The way to obtain Him, gain Him, experience Him, and enjoy Him is to deny whatever we are, whatever we have, and whatever we can do. Do not bring anything to Christ. He does not need what you are or have, but you need Him. In every way Christ wants to replace you with Himself. Christ has already obtained us that we may obtain Him. Now He is waiting for us to experience Him and enjoy Him by denying all things and by counting all things loss for His sake. (*The Experience of Christ,* pp. 75-76)

Today's Reading

If we want to participate in Christ, experience Christ, and enjoy Christ, we must repudiate our flesh. The greatest obstacle to enjoying Christ is our natural heritage. For example, the greatest hindrance for a naturally gentle brother to enjoy Christ is his gentleness, for he may repudiate all things except his gentleness. Although we have enjoyed Christ to a certain degree, we all have been frustrated and hindered by our natural heritage. It is the good flesh that is the greatest hindrance to experiencing Christ and enjoying Him.

Suppose a certain person is naturally eloquent and makes a great impact upon an audience. If he becomes a Christian, he can be an outstanding preacher and draw a great crowd. Being naturally eloquent, he can be influential and have a great impact. But there will be no need for Christ or for the Spirit. With his natural eloquence, he can secure a large following. If I were such an eloquent speaker, you all would appreciate me. You would praise the Lord that such a brother had been brought into the Lord's recovery. However, it is difficult for such an eloquent speaker to enjoy Christ in his speaking because he has no need of Christ.

Suppose another person is not born with the ability to speak eloquently. On the contrary, he is slow and halting in his expression. Whenever he speaks more than a few minutes, everyone falls asleep. Suppose he gets saved, loves the Lord and the church, and has a burden to speak a word for the Lord. Having no trust in himself, he spontaneously repudiates himself and puts all his trust in Christ. He may fast and pray desperately to the Lord, saying, "Lord, if You don't speak, I will not be able to speak. If You don't do something with my speaking, I am finished." When he stands up to speak, he is in fear and trembling. But because he has repudiated himself, he experiences Christ and enjoys Christ as he speaks.

No matter whether we are dull or intelligent, we must reject all that we are. Nothing natural should be allowed to replace Christ. Any naturally good thing will frustrate us from the enjoyment of Christ. (*The Experience of Christ,* pp. 73-74)

Further Reading: The Experience of Christ, ch. 8; Life-study of Philippians, msgs. 18-22

Enlightenment and inspiration: _____

_____

_____

Hymns, #1025

1   Give up the world, Christ to obtain,
      He is your heart's very need;
    What else can you desire or seek?
      All things are empty indeed!

      He is so rich, He is so full,
        He can fulfill all your needs!
      He is so good, He is so sweet,
        All your desire He exceeds!

2   Give up the world, Christ to obtain,
      He is the One you require;
    Once you receive this glorious Christ,
      Never the rest you'll desire.

3   Though very great is all the world,
      And very small is your heart,
    Yet the great world with all its wealth
      Never can fill your small heart.

4   If you have Christ, you have all joys;
      Without this Christ, only pains;
    Where there is Christ there morning is;
      Where He is not, night remains.

Composition for prophecy with main point and sub-points: _____

_____

_____

_____

_____

_____

_____

_____

_____

_____

_____

_____

_____

_____

_____

_____

_____

_____

_____

_____

_____

_____

_____

_____

_____

_____

_____

_____

_____

_____

_____

_____

_____

_____

Taking Christ as Our Goal (2)
Knowing Christ, the Power of His Resurrection, and the Fellowship of His Sufferings

Scripture Reading: Phil. 3:10

Day 1   **I. Paul aspired to know Christ (Phil. 3:10):**

A. To have the excellency of the knowledge of Christ in Philippians 3:8 is by revelation, but to know Him in verse 10 is by experience.

B. Paul first received the revelation of Christ, then sought the experience of Christ—to know and enjoy Christ in an experiential way.

C. *The one thing* in the book of Philippians is the subjective knowledge and experience of Christ (2:2; cf. 1:20-21; 2:5; 3:7-9; 4:12-13).

D. To know Christ is not merely to have the knowledge concerning Him but to gain His very person (2 Cor. 2:10; cf. Col. 2:9, 16-17):

Day 2   1. To gain something requires the paying of a price; to gain Christ is to experience, enjoy, and take possession of all His unsearchable riches (Eph. 3:8) by paying a price.

2. Christ has gained us, taken possession of us, that we might gain Him, take possession of Him (Phil. 3:12).

3. The Christian life is a life of gaining Christ in His full ministry in His three divine and mystical stages—incarnation, inclusion, and intensification (John 1:14; 1 Cor. 15:45b; Rev. 1:4; 4:5; 5:6):

a. Even though Paul had experienced and gained Christ tremendously, he did not consider that he had experienced Him in full or gained Him to the uttermost; for this reason he was still advancing toward the goal—the gaining of Christ to the fullest extent (Phil. 3:12-14).

b. In order to gain Christ to the fullest extent, Paul not only forsook his experiences in Judaism but also would not linger in his past experiences of Christ and be limited by them; he forgot the past (v. 13).

c. Not to forget but to linger in our past experiences, however genuine they were, frustrates our further pursuing of Christ (v. 13; Heb. 6:1a).

d. Christ is unsearchably rich, and there is a vast territory of His riches to be possessed; Paul was stretching out to reach the farthest extent of this territory (Phil. 3:13).

Day 3

II. Paul aspired to know the power of Christ's resurrection (v. 10):

A. The power of Christ's resurrection is His resurrection life, which raised Him from the dead (Eph. 1:19-20).

B. The Spirit is the reality of Christ's resurrection and its power (Rom. 8:9-11; 1 Cor. 15:45b; 1 John 5:6).

C. The Spirit compounded with Christ's resurrection and its power (Phil. 1:19; Exo. 30:23-25) indwells our spirit (Rom. 8:10-11) to dispense Christ's resurrection and its power not only to our spirit and soul (vv. 6b, 10) but also to our mortal body (vv. 11, 13b; 2 Cor. 4:11).

D. We should cooperate with the resurrecting Spirit to recognize that we have been resurrected with Christ (Col. 2:12; Eph. 2:6a) and to pursue the power of the resurrection of Christ:

Day 4

1. It is by this power of Christ's resurrection that we, the lovers of Christ, determine to take the cross by denying our self (Matt. 16:24; cf. S. S. 2:8-9).

2. It is also by this power of resurrection that we, the lovers of Christ, are enabled to be

conformed to His death, to be one with His cross (Phil. 3:10; cf. S. S. 2:14-15).

3. In order to experience the life-giving Spirit as the reality of the flourishing riches of the resurrection of Christ, we have to discern our spirit from our soul (Heb. 4:12; cf. S. S. 2:14-15).

E. Christ's resurrection with its power in the life-giving Spirit is the sufficient grace of the processed and consummated Triune God (2 Cor. 12:9; 13:14; 1 Cor. 15:10, 45b, 58; cf. Exo. 3:2-6, 14-15).

Day 5 **III. Paul aspired to know the fellowship of Christ's sufferings (Phil. 3:10):**

A. With Christ, the sufferings and death came first, followed by the resurrection; with us, the power of His resurrection comes first, followed by the participation in His sufferings and conformity to His death.

B. We first receive the power of His resurrection; then by this power we are enabled to participate in His sufferings and live a crucified life in conformity to His death.

C. Christ's sufferings are of two categories: those for accomplishing redemption, which were completed by Christ Himself, and those for producing and building the church, which need to be filled up by the apostles and the believers (Col. 1:24):

1. We cannot participate in Christ's sufferings for redemption, but we must take part in the sufferings of Christ for the producing and building up of the Body (cf. Rev. 1:9; 2 Tim. 2:10; 2 Cor. 1:5-6; 4:12; 6:8-11).

Day 6 2. Christ as the Lamb of God suffered for redemption (John 1:29); Christ as the grain of wheat suffered for reproducing and building (12:24):

a. The Lord, as a grain of wheat that fell into the ground, lost His soul-life through death that He might release His eternal life in resurrection to the many grains (10:10-11).

b. The one grain did not complete all the sufferings that are needed for the building up of the Body; as the many grains, we must suffer in the same way the one grain suffered (12:24-26):

1) As the many grains, we also must lose our soul-life through death that we may enjoy eternal life in resurrection (v. 25).

2) This is to follow Him that we may serve Him and walk with Him on this way, the way of losing our soul-life and living in His resurrection (v. 26).

3) The way for the church to come into being and to increase is not by human glory; it is by the death of the cross (vv. 20-24).

Morning Nourishment

Phil. **But moreover I also count all things to be loss on**
3:8 **account of the excellency of the knowledge of**
Christ Jesus my Lord, on account of whom I have
suffered the loss of all things and count *them* as
refuse that I may gain Christ.

10 **To know Him and the power of His resurrection**
and the fellowship of His sufferings, being con-
formed to His death.

We should know Christ not only by revelation, thus having the excellency of the knowledge of Christ. We need to know Him also by enjoying Him, by experiencing Him, by being one with Him, and by having Him live within us and walk with us. In this way we know Him not merely in an objective way, but much more in a subjective way. Thus, we know Him both by revelation and by experience. Eventually, He becomes us and we become Him. This enables us to say with Paul, "To me, to live is Christ" (Phil. 1:21). We shall also be able to say that Christ is being magnified in us. This is the book of Philippians. This book reveals how to know Christ in an experiential way. It tells how to know Him, the power of His resurrection, and the fellowship of His sufferings. As we know Him in this way, we can say, "Christ is being magnified in me. For to me, to live is Christ." Then we shall go on to say, "Oh, that I may gain Christ and be found in Him!" Eventually,...we shall be able to say, "I am able to do all things in Him who empowers me" (Phil. 4:13). (*The Experience of Christ,* p. 146)

Today's Reading

Paul lived in a condition of not having his own righteousness but having the righteousness of God, in order to know (to experience) Christ and the power of His resurrection and the fellowship of His sufferings. To have the excellency of the knowledge of Christ in Philippians 3:8 is by revelation. But to know Him in verse 10 is by experience—to have the experiential knowledge of Him, to experience Him in the full knowledge of Him. Paul first received the revelation of Christ and then sought for the experience of Christ—to know and enjoy Him in an experiential way.

After we receive the excellency of the knowledge of Christ, we shall be willing to suffer the loss of all things and count them as refuse in order to gain Christ and be found in Him. As a result, we shall know Christ experientially. Therefore, verse 9 comes out of verse 8, and verse 10 comes out of verse 9. If we do not have the excellency of the knowledge of Christ (v. 8), we shall not be found in Christ, for it is having the excellency of the knowledge of Christ which makes us willing to suffer the loss of all things and count them as refuse in order to gain Christ and be found in Him. Then, once we have gained Christ and are found in Him, we shall know Him; that is, we shall enjoy Him and experience Him.

To gain Christ is one thing, and to experience Him is another. We may illustrate this difference by the difference between buying groceries and eating food which has been purchased and prepared. Gaining Christ may be compared to buying groceries, and the experience of Christ may be compared to the eating of the food we have first purchased and cooked. However, before we buy any groceries, we must first have the excellency of the knowledge of groceries. Before we purchase anything, we are first attracted by the excellency of the knowledge of that thing. Thus, first we have the excellency of the knowledge of the groceries, then we gain them by buying them, and finally we enjoy the food by eating it. In like manner, Paul first received the excellency of the knowledge of Christ, then he paid the price to gain Christ and be found in Him, and finally he experienced Christ and enjoyed Him. Paul realized that to gain Christ and be found in Him always results in knowing Him, in enjoying and experiencing Him. (*Life-study of Philippians*, pp. 171-173)

Further Reading: The Experience of Christ, ch. 16; Life-study of Philippians, msg. 21; How to Be a Co-worker and an Elder and How to Fulfill Their Obligations, ch. 1

Enlightenment and inspiration: _____

_____

Morning Nourishment

Phil.
3:12-14

Not that I have already obtained or am already perfected, but I pursue, if even I may lay hold of that for which I also have been laid hold of by Christ Jesus. Brothers, I do not account of myself to have laid hold; but one thing *I do:* Forgetting the things which are behind and stretching forward to the things which are before, I pursue toward the goal for the prize to which God in Christ Jesus has called *me* upward.

The Lord has taken possession of us so that we might take possession of Him. This was His purpose in grasping us. Christ wants us to gain Him. The Lord's aim in His salvation is to seize us that we might take full possession of Him. Not even when Paul was writing to the Philippians did he regard himself as having gained Christ in a full way. Rather, he was still pursuing Christ in order to gain Him.

In Philippians 3 Paul uses three Greek words that are rendered *gain, obtained,* and *laid hold of.* The meaning of these words is very close, for to obtain is to gain, and to gain is to lay hold of. The strongest of these expressions is *lay hold of.* Christ has laid hold of us that we might lay hold of Him. He has gained us that we might gain Him. Thus, the Christian life is a life of gaining Christ. How much have you gained of Christ? This is a crucial question. We grow in life by gaining Christ. The degree to which we have gained Christ is the degree to which we have grown with Christ. We all need to gain Christ in order to grow in life. Spiritual growth is measured by how much we have gained of Christ.

I hope that the saints will use 3:12 to improve their vocabulary concerning conversion and salvation. According to this verse, conversion means that Christ gains a person so that this person may gain Him. Gaining Christ is a life-long matter. Day by day our goal should be to gain Him. Even during his imprisonment, Paul was pursuing Christ in order to gain Him. (*Life-study of Philippians,* pp. 192-193)

Today's Reading

Even though Paul had experienced and gained Christ tremendously, he did not consider that he had experienced Him in full or gained Him to the uttermost [3:13]. For this reason he was still advancing toward the goal—the gaining of Christ to the fullest extent.

In verse 13 Paul speaks of forgetting the things behind. In order to gain Christ to the fullest extent, Paul not only forsook his experience in Judaism but also refused to dwell on his past experiences of Christ and be limited by them. To dwell on our past experiences, no matter how real they may have been, frustrates our further pursuing after Christ.

In verse 13 Paul tells us that he was stretching forward to the things which are before. He knew that Christ is unsearchably rich, that there is a vast territory of His riches to be possessed. He was stretching forward to gain these riches and to advance further into this territory.

Paul was pursuing toward the goal for the prize. Christ is both the goal and the prize. The goal is the fullest enjoyment and gain of Christ, and the prize is the uttermost enjoyment of Christ in the millennial kingdom as a reward to the victorious runners of the New Testament race. In order to reach the goal for the prize, Paul was exercised to forget the things which are behind and to stretch forward to the things which are before. This is the way to gain Christ by pursuing Him.

Even though Paul was a matured saint and a very experienced apostle, he tells us that he had not already obtained and had not yet been perfected. He did not regard himself as one who had obtained the full enjoyment of Christ or the full maturity in life. He, of course, had obtained the common salvation by the common faith (1 Tim. 1:14-16), but he was still pursuing Christ in order to gain Him. (*Life-study of Philippians,* pp. 193-194)

Further Reading: Life-study of Philippians, msgs. 23, 52

Enlightenment and inspiration: _____

_____

Morning Nourishment

1 Cor. 15:45 ...The last Adam *became* a life-giving Spirit.

Rom. 8:11 And if the Spirit of the One who raised Jesus from the dead dwells in you, He who raised Christ Jesus from the dead will also give life to your mortal bodies through His Spirit who indwells you.

Eph. 2:6 And raised *us* up together with *Him*...

2 Cor. 4:16 Therefore we do not lose heart; but though our outer man is decaying, yet our inner *man* is being renewed day by day.

The Christian life is a life in Christ's resurrection. To know the Spirit, we have to know resurrection. Resurrection is the Triune God consummated to be the life-giving Spirit. We are not able to understand such a deep and high mystery, the mystery of resurrection, but we can experience resurrection. We do not even understand our human life, but we can experience this life daily. When we eat food, we take in many nourishing elements and vitamins which we do not understand, yet we can enjoy them. We do not know what human life is, but we can surely enjoy this life.

Who can fully understand the Triune God? We cannot understand the Triune God, but He is available for us to experience and enjoy. Nearly every morning, my first prayer is somewhat like this: "Thank You, Lord, for the peace. Thank You for the safety. Thank You for Your presence. Thank You for Your cleansing. Thank You for Your forgiveness. Thank You for Your preserving of my health." This is a simple prayer, but through this simple prayer, I enjoy the Triune God and I am filled with the Spirit. I have been enjoying the Triune God for close to seventy years. I cannot deny there is a God, because day by day I enjoy Him as resurrection. (*The Christian Life*, pp. 111-112)

Today's Reading

In order to experience resurrection, we also need to be limited in our speaking. The more we gossip, the more resurrection is gone. The more we gossip, the more there is no Spirit in our experience. To experience the Spirit as the reality of resurrection, we need to turn to our spirit to pray, praise, sing, or talk to God. The title of Psalm 18 indicates that this psalm was David's conversation with God, his talk to God. We need to talk to God and consult with Him. After ten minutes of talking to God, we will be on fire and full of the Spirit as the reality of resurrection.

The Spirit is the reality of Christ's resurrection and its power, with which the Spirit has been compounded (1 John 5:6).

The Spirit compounded with Christ's resurrection and its power indwells our spirit (Rom. 8:11) to dispense Christ's resurrection and its power not only to our spirit and soul (Rom. 8:6b, 10; 2 Cor. 4:16), but also to our mortal body (Rom. 8:11; 2 Cor. 4:11).

We should cooperate with the resurrecting Spirit to recognize that we have been resurrected with Christ (Col. 2:12; Eph. 2:6a) and to pursue the power of the resurrection of Christ (Phil. 3:10a). Paul said that he wanted to know Christ and the power of His resurrection. This power will conform us to Christ's death (Phil. 3:10b; 2 Cor. 4:10, 16).

The more we die, the more Spirit we have. The more we die, the more we are in resurrection. The more we die, the more the divine attributes, such as peace, joy, light, life, and love, will be with us to be the content of our human virtues. This is the Christian life, and this is the great mystery of godliness (1 Tim. 3:16). Godliness is the living out of the Triune God, the very manifestation of the divine Being in our flesh.

We need to be people who are occupied with the Triune God, with the consummated Spirit, and with the resurrection. We need to be "crazy" Christians who are filled with the Spirit inwardly and outwardly. We should be fully in resurrection. What is resurrection? Resurrection is the processed, consummated Triune God as the compound Spirit. (*The Christian Life*, pp. 113-114)

Further Reading: The Christian Life, msgs. 7, 10; The Experience and Growth in Life, msg. 12

Enlightenment and inspiration: _____
_____
_____
_____

Morning Nourishment

Heb. For the word of God is living and operative and
4:12 sharper than any two-edged sword, and piercing
even to the dividing of soul and spirit and of
joints and marrow, and able to discern the
thoughts and intentions of the heart.

1 Cor. But by the grace of God I am what I am; and His
15:10 grace unto me did not turn out to be in vain, but,
on the contrary, I labored more abundantly than
all of them, yet not I but the grace of God which
is with me.

S. S. The voice of my beloved! Now he comes, leaping
2:8 upon the mountains, skipping upon the hills.

14 My dove, in the clefts of the rock, in the covert of
the precipice, let me see your countenance, let
me hear your voice; for your voice is sweet, and
your countenance is lovely.

Christ's resurrection with its power in the life-giving
Spirit is the sufficient grace of the processed and consum-
mated Triune God (2 Cor. 12:9; 13:14; 1 Cor. 15:10, 45b, 58).
We may also say that the Spirit as the realization of
Christ's resurrection and its power is the sufficient grace.
The sufficient grace is the compound Spirit as the reality of
resurrection.

First Corinthians 15 proves this. This is a long chapter of
fifty-eight verses on Christ's resurrection. In this chapter,
Paul presents a rebuttal to those who say there is no resurrection (vv. 12-19). In verse 10a Paul also said, "But by the
grace of God I am what I am." Grace here is the resurrected Christ as the life-giving Spirit. Paul went on to say, "I
labored more abundantly than all of them, yet not I but the
grace of God which is with me" (v. 10b). Paul labored more
abundantly than all of the apostles by the grace which
operated in him. The grace of God with him was the consummated Spirit, the consummation of the Triune God. (*The
Christian Life*, p. 114)

Today's Reading

In order to empower and encourage His lover to rise up and get away from her down situation in her introspection of the self, Christ empowers her by showing her the power of His resurrection by the gazelle's leaping upon the mountains and the young hart's skipping upon the hills (S. S. 2:8-9). It is by this power of Christ's resurrection that we, the lovers of Christ, determine to take the cross by denying our self (Matt. 16:24). Have we ever had such a determination? Often we forget what we determined to do before God. We need to be reminded. It is also by this power of Christ's resurrection that we, the lovers of Christ, are enabled to be conformed to His death (Phil. 3:10), to be one with His cross as staying in the clefts of the rock, in the covert of the precipice (S. S. 2:14).

Christ encourages His seeker by the flourishing riches of His resurrection (2:11-13). The dormant days (winter) are past and the trials (rain) are over and gone. The life in all appearances is blossoming. The time of praising—singing—has come. The fruit tree has ripened in its fruits, and the vines are in blossom, giving forth their fragrance. This is a portrait of the riches of Christ's resurrection.

In order to experience the life-giving Spirit as the reality of resurrection in our spirit, we have to discern our spirit from our soul. In our soul we are the old man (Eph. 4:22), the soulish man, the natural man (1 Cor. 2:14). In our spirit we are the new man (Eph. 4:24), the spiritual man (1 Cor. 2:14-15), that lives and walks in our spirit as God's Holiest of all, indwelt by and mingled with the life-giving Spirit, the pneumatic Christ. It is in such a mingled spirit that we participate in and experience the resurrection of Christ, the reality of which is the all-inclusive, life-giving, compound Spirit, the consummation of the processed and consummated Triune God. (*Crystallization-study of Song of Songs*, pp. 67-69)

Further Reading: The Christian Life, ch. 10; Crystallization-study of Song of Songs, msgs. 5-6

Enlightenment and inspiration: _____

_____

_____

Morning Nourishment

Phil. **To know Him and the power of His resurrection**
3:10 **and the fellowship of His sufferings, being con-**
       formed to His death.
Col. **I now rejoice in my sufferings on your behalf and**
1:24 **fill up on my part that which is lacking of the**
       afflictions of Christ in my flesh for His Body,
       which is the church.

The participation in Christ's suffering—"the fellowship of His sufferings"—(Matt. 20:22-23; Col. 1:24) is a necessary condition for the experience of the power of His resurrection (2 Tim. 2:11) by being conformed to His death. Paul was pursuing to know and experience not only the excellency of Christ Himself, but also the life power of His resurrection and the participation in His sufferings. With Christ, the sufferings and death came first, followed by the resurrection. With us, the power of His resurrection comes first, then the fellowship of His sufferings and conformity to His death. We first receive the power of His resurrection. Then by this power we are enabled to participate in His sufferings and live a crucified life in conformity to His death. Such sufferings are mainly for producing and building up the Body of Christ.

In order to experience Christ, we must be in the power of resurrection. We cannot be in our natural life. The more we know the power of Christ's resurrection, the more we shall participate in the sufferings of Christ and thereby have the fellowship of His sufferings. If we experience the fellowship of Christ's sufferings, we shall then be conformed to His death. As we are conformed to the death of Christ, we are ushered into the power of His resurrection. It is by this resurrection power that we know Christ and experience Him. (*Life-study of Philippians,* pp. 175-176)

Today's Reading

We go on from the power of resurrection to the fellowship of Christ's sufferings. Although it is wonderful to enjoy the power of Christ's resurrection, the power of resurrection is not mainly for our enjoyment. In God's economy there is no selfish enjoyment. The power of Christ's resurrection is for the producing and the building up of the Body. God's intention is not to express Himself through certain individuals; it is to express Himself through a Body composed of many believers. Thus, the expression of God in man is not an individual matter, but a corporate matter. If we put ourselves aside and remain under the death of the cross, we shall enjoy the power of resurrection. Immediately, the power of resurrection will produce the Body. This goal of producing and building up the Body stirs up opposition. Satan knows of this goal, and he stirs up opposition against it. The goal of building the Body always arouses opposition. When the opposition comes, we suffer. In this way we enter into the fellowship of Christ's sufferings.

Philippians 3:10 speaks of knowing Christ, of knowing the power of His resurrection, and then of knowing the fellowship of His sufferings. According to Colossians 1:24, these sufferings are for the Body. In this verse Paul says, "I now rejoice in my sufferings on your behalf and fill up on my part that which is lacking of the afflictions of Christ in my flesh for His Body, which is the church." When I was young, I was troubled by this verse. I said, "Christ's afflictions have been completed. How can Paul say that there was something lacking in Christ's afflictions?" I honestly thought that Paul was wrong. How can we say that anything related to Christ is not complete? Nevertheless, the Bible reveals that there is something lacking in the afflictions of Christ. Although everything else related to Christ is complete, His afflictions are not complete. (*The Experience of Christ,* pp. 142-143)

Further Reading: Life-study of Philippians, msgs. 21, 52;
   The Experience of Christ, ch. 16; *Life and Building as Portrayed in the Song of Songs,* chs. 11, 13*

Enlightenment and inspiration: _____

_____

_____

Morning Nourishment

John
1:29 The next day he saw Jesus coming to him and said, Behold, the Lamb of God, who takes away the sin of the world!

12:24 Truly, truly, I say to you, Unless the grain of wheat falls into the ground and dies, it abides alone; but if it dies, it bears much fruit.

2 Tim.
2:10 Therefore I endure all things for the sake of the chosen ones, that they themselves also may obtain the salvation which is in Christ Jesus with eternal glory.

At this point we need to differentiate between two kinds of sufferings, the sufferings of Christ and the sufferings that come from our mistakes. Do not think that all the sufferings you undergo are for the building up of the Body. For example,...if you make an error in your financial records and find yourself several hundred dollars in debt, that is...the suffering caused by error, not the suffering Christ. However, suppose on your job you enjoy the power of Christ's resurrection. Because of this, certain of your superiors oppose you, either passing you up for a promotion or causing you to be dismissed from your job. This suffering may be counted as the suffering of Christ for the producing and building up of the Body. Thus, one category of suffering is due to our mistakes and wrongdoings, and the other results from our testimony.

When we set ourselves aside and experience the power of resurrection, our testimony will be very strong. This will arouse the opposition of the enemy, and we shall suffer. This kind of suffering is the suffering of Christ. We all need to know the fellowship of Christ's sufferings, the sufferings that make up what is lacking of Christ's sufferings for the building up of the Body. This should be not merely doctrine, but an experience in which we enjoy Christ. (*The Experience of Christ*, pp. 144-145)

Today's Reading

Christ's sufferings have accomplished two things. First, His sufferings have accomplished redemption. Without suffering, Christ could not redeem us. Second, His sufferings have also accomplished the producing and building up of the church. Thus, within His great sufferings, there is a part for redemption and a part for the producing and building up of the church. ...[While on the cross], Christ became sin in the eyes of God (2 Cor. 5:21), for God gathered all of man's sin, placed it upon Him, and condemned Him. That was the reason the Lord cried out, "My God, My God, why have You forsaken Me?" (Matt. 27:46)....When He was made sin, He suffered God's judgment and condemnation. This was Christ's greatest suffering, and through it He accomplished redemption. It is impossible for us to share in this aspect of Christ's sufferings. If we say that we can share in this aspect, we blaspheme. He alone suffered God's judgment on the cross for the accomplishment of redemption.

However, Christ suffered not only for redemption but also for the producing of the Body. In the Gospel of John Christ is described as the Lamb of God who takes away the sin of the world (John 1:29). But He is also presented as the grain of wheat that fell into the earth to produce many grains (John 12:24). The Lamb suffered for redemption, whereas the grain suffered for reproducing. Although we cannot share in Christ's sufferings for redemption, we can share in His sufferings for reproducing and for building up the Body. Christ was the one grain, and we are the many grains. As the many grains, we must suffer in the same way the one grain suffered. The one grain did not complete all the sufferings that are needed for the building up of the Body. For this, there is something lacking, and the lack must be made up by you and me. There is a portion for each of us to make up.

When we put ourselves aside and remain under the cross, the power of resurrection will be our portion. Immediately opposition will rise up against us, and we shall suffer. This suffering is in the fellowship of the sufferings of Christ for the building up of the Body. (*The Experience of Christ*, pp. 143-144)

Further Reading: The Experience of Christ, ch. 16; Life-study of John, msg. 26; Life-study of Colossians, msg. 12

Enlightenment and inspiration: _____
_____

Hymns, #481

1   Crucified with Christ my Savior,
    To the world and self and sin;
    To the death-born life of Jesus
    I am sweetly ent'ring in:
    In His fellowship of suff'ring,
    To His death conformed to be,
    I am going with my Savior
      All the way to Calvary.

    All the way to Calvary,
    Where my Savior went for me,
    Help me, Lord, to go with Thee,
    All the way to Calvary.

2   'Tis not hard to die with Christ
    When His risen life we know;
    'Tis not hard to share His suff'rings
    When our hearts with joy o'erflow.
    In His resurrection power
    He has come to dwell in me,
    And my heart is gladly going
      All the way to Calvary.

3   If we die we'll live with Christ,
    If we suffer we shall reign;
    Only thus the prize of glory
    Can the conqueror attain.
    Oh, how sweet, on that glad morning
    Should the Master say to thee,
    "Yes, my child, thou didst go with me
      All the way to Calvary."

Composition for prophecy with main point and sub-points: _____

_____

_____

_____

_____

_____

_____

_____

_____

_____

_____

_____

_____

_____

_____

_____

_____

_____

_____

_____

_____

_____

_____

_____

_____

_____

_____

_____

_____

_____

_____

_____

_____

_____

Taking Christ as Our Goal (3)
Being Conformed to Christ's Death and
Attaining to the Out-resurrection

Scripture Reading: Phil. 3:10-11

Day 1

I. In Philippians 3:10 Paul spoke of "being conformed to His death"; this expression indicates that Paul desired to take Christ's death as the mold of his life:

A. The excellency of the knowledge of Christ, counting all things as loss, gaining Christ, being found in Him, knowing Him, knowing the power of His resurrection, and knowing the fellowship of His sufferings all issue in one thing—being conformed to Christ's death (vv. 7-10).

B. Being conformed to Christ's death is the base of the experience of Christ (1:20-21a; 3:9-10).

C. The mold of Christ's death refers to the continual putting to death of His natural, human life that He might live by the life of God (John 6:57a):

1. When the Lord Jesus was on earth, He lived a crucified life; by living a crucified life He was alive to God and lived Him.

2. He always put His human life to death so that the divine life within Him could flow out (10:10b-11, 17).

3. As He was living, He was also dying—dying to the old creation in order to live a life in the new creation; this is the meaning of "His death" in Philippians 3:10.

Day 2

D. Christ's death is a mold to which we are conformed in much the same way that dough is put into a cake mold and conformed to it:

1. God has put us into the mold of Christ's death, and day by day God is molding us to conform us to this death (Rom. 6:3-4).

2. Our life should be conformed to such a mold—dying to our human life in order to live the divine life (Gal. 2:20; 2 Cor. 4:10-11).

3. If we put to death our natural life, we shall have the consciousness that we have another life, the divine life, within us; this life will be released, and then in our experience we shall be conformed to Christ's death (John 10:10b; 1 John 5:11-12).

4. In the mold of Christ's death the natural man is killed, the old man is crucified, and the self is nullified (2 Cor. 4:16; Rom. 6:6; Matt. 16:24).

5. If we allow our circumstances to press us into this mold, our daily life will be molded into the form of Christ's death (Rom. 8:28-29).

6. We are conformed to the mold of Christ's death by the power of Christ's resurrection (Phil. 3:10; John 11:25; Eph. 1:19-20; S. S. 2:8-13).

Day 3

E. As we are conformed to Christ's death, we experience His all-accomplishing death:

1. By being conformed to His death, we experience Christ in His death for the release, impartation, and multiplication of life (John 12:24-26; 2 Cor. 4:12).

2. The only way to glorify God is to be conformed to Christ's death; the more we are conformed to Christ's death, the more we glorify the Father (John 12:28; 13:31).

3. When we die the death of Christ and are conformed to His death, we shall be a magnet drawing others to Christ (12:32).

4. The more we die with Christ, the more we save our soul (v. 25).

5. If we are willing to be conformed to Christ's death, we shall overcome the world and defeat Satan (v. 31; Heb. 2:14).

Day 4

II. **The result of being conformed to Christ's death is that we may attain to, or arrive at, the out-resurrection from the dead (Phil. 3:11):**

A. The out-resurrection is the outstanding resurrection, the extra-resurrection, which will be a prize to the overcoming saints (Rev. 20:4, 6):

1. All believers who are dead in Christ will participate in the resurrection from the dead at the Lord's coming back (1 Thes. 4:16; 1 Cor. 15:52).

2. The Lord's overcomers will enjoy an extra, outstanding portion of that resurrection, a resurrection in which they will receive the reward of the kingdom; this is what the apostle Paul sought after (Heb. 11:35, 26).

3. The out-resurrection should be the goal and destination of our Christian life (Phil. 3:11-15a).

Day 5

B. To attain to the out-resurrection means that our entire being is gradually and continually resurrected (1 Thes. 5:23):

1. God first resurrected our deadened spirit; He proceeds to resurrect our soul and our mortal body until our whole being—spirit, soul, and body—is fully resurrected out of our old being by His life and with His life (Eph. 2:5-6; Rom. 8:6, 11).

2. If we are conformed to Christ's death, every part of our being will be gradually resurrected; thus, the Christian life is a process of resurrection.

C. The out-resurrection is a resurrection out of the old creation into the new creation (Gal. 6:15; 2 Cor. 5:17):

1. To be in the out-resurrection means to leave everything of the old creation and to be brought into God.

2. In the out-resurrection there is no element of the old creation; instead, everything is full of the divine element (Rev. 21:5a).

Day 6

D. For Paul to live was Christ as the out-resurrection (Phil. 1:21a; 3:11):

1. The out-resurrection is actually the dear, precious, excellent person of Christ, the One who, through crucifixion and resurrection, has passed out of the old creation and has entered into God (John 14:3, 20; Heb. 6:19-20).

2. The Christ whom we should live is Himself the out-resurrection (Phil. 1:21a; 3:11; John 11:25).

E. We need to be conformed to Christ's death so that by any means we may attain to the out-resurrection from the dead; this is the only way for the Lord to go on in His recovery, the only way for the Lord to build up His church, the only way to prepare the bride, and the only way to bring the Lord back (Phil. 3:10-11; Matt. 16:18; Rev. 19:7-9a; 22:14, 20).

Morning Nourishment

Phil. To know Him and the power of His resurrection
3:10 and the fellowship of His sufferings, being conformed to His death.

John As the living Father has sent Me and I live
6:57 because of the Father...

10:10-11 ...I have come that they may have life and may
have *it* abundantly. I am the good Shepherd; the
good Shepherd lays down His life for the sheep.

[Philippians 3:10] indicates that Paul desired to take
Christ's death as the mold of his life. Christ's death is a
mold to which we are conformed in much the same way that
dough is put into a cake mold and conformed to it. Paul
continually lived a crucified life, a life under the cross, just
as Christ did in His human living. Through such a life the
resurrection power is experienced and expressed. The mold
of Christ's death refers to the continual putting to death of
His human life that He might live by the life of God (John
6:57). Our life should be conformed to such a mold—dying
to our human life in order to live the divine life. Being
conformed to the death of Christ is the condition for knowing and experiencing Him, the power of His resurrection,
and the fellowship of His sufferings. (*The Conclusion of the
New Testament,* p. 1549)

Today's Reading

When the Lord Jesus was on earth, He lived a crucified
life. Christ had two lives—the divine life and the human life.
It was God's desire that the man Jesus live the divine life
by means of His human life. God did not want Him simply
to live out the human life. Rather, it was God's intention
that the Lord Jesus live the divine life through the channel
of the human life.

This kind of living can be illustrated by what happens
when a branch from one tree is grafted into another tree.
The branch that has been grafted into the tree does not live

out its own life; instead, it lives the life of the tree into which it has been grafted. This means that the life of the tree flows out through the branch which has been grafted into it.

When the Lord Jesus was on earth, He always put His human life to death so that the divine life within Him could be lived out. This is the pattern of Christ's death. In the eyes of man, the Lord Jesus was crucified at the end of His ministry. But in the eyes of God, He was crucified throughout His life on earth. This is proved by the fact that He was baptized when He came forth to minister, as an indication that He had put Himself into death. The Lord's baptism by John indicated that He was living His human life under the killing power of the cross. His was a life in which the human life was crucified, so that the divine life could be lived out. What a wonderful living the Lord Jesus had!

This wonderful living implies the pattern of Christ's death. According to this pattern, Christ continually put to death His human life so that His divine life could flow out. This is the mold of the life of Christ and the death of Christ.

There can be no doubt that the human life of the Lord Jesus was excellent. But even such an excellent human life was put to death for the sake of the release of the divine life. Please pay attention to the fact that the Lord's human life was not put to death because it was wrong in some way; it was put to death so that the divine life could be lived out. This was the reason the Lord's human life had to be rejected, broken, and put to death. The principle should be the same with us today. As those who believe in Christ and who have been regenerated by the Spirit, we have both the human life and the divine life. No matter how good our human life may be, it must be put to death if the divine life is to be lived out. (*Life-study of Philippians,* pp. 185-186)

Further Reading: The Conclusion of the New Testament, msg. 143; *Life-study of Philippians,* msgs. 22, 53; *The Experience of Christ,* chs. 7, 14-21

Enlightenment and inspiration: _____

_____

_____

Morning Nourishment

Rom. Or are you ignorant that all of us who have been
6:3-4 baptized into Christ Jesus have been baptized
into His death? We have been buried therefore
with Him through baptism into His death, in order
that just as Christ was raised from the dead
through the glory of the Father, so also we might
walk in newness of life.

2 Cor. Always bearing about in the body the putting to
4:10-11 death of Jesus that the life of Jesus also may be
manifested in our body. For we who are alive are
always being delivered unto death for Jesus' sake
that the life of Jesus also may be manifested in our
mortal flesh.

According to Philippians 3:10 and 11, we firstly have the power of resurrection, secondly the conformity to Christ's death, and thirdly the attaining unto the out-resurrection. Thus, the sequence is resurrection, death, resurrection. In our experience, which comes first, death or resurrection? We have already pointed out that death is the threshold of resurrection. Therefore, death must be first. But in these verses resurrection comes before death. Romans 6 says that we are baptized into Christ's death and indicates that the power of resurrection follows death. In Philippians 3 death is implied by the fact that Paul counted all things loss. Paul's counting all things loss was actually his experience of remaining in the death of Christ. Because he remained in death, the power of Christ's resurrection could rise up in him. This is the way to know the power of resurrection. (*The Experience of Christ*, p. 196)

Today's Reading

The way to know the life power in a grain of wheat is to put that grain into the soil and keep it there. Likewise, in order to know Christ as the power of resurrection life within us, we need to remain in Christ's death. As we remain in His death, the power of life will rise up. When the power of life rises up, it will bring us into deeper death. This deeper death is the conformity to Christ's death.

The day we were baptized we were merely put into Christ's death; we were not yet conformed to it. For example, when sisters bake a cake, they put the dough into a mold. But after the dough is put into the mold, it is pressed and processed until it conforms to the mold. Thus, to put the dough into the mold is one thing, and to conform it to the mold is another. When we were baptized, we were put into the death of Christ, but we were not molded to the form of His death. When we are willing to remain in His death, the power of resurrection will rise up within us and bring us deeper and deeper into death. This is not being baptized into His death, but being conformed to His death. We need to say, "Lord, how I thank You for Your wonderful death. To stay here is not a suffering. How sweet and pleasant it is to remain in Your death! When someone gives me a difficult time, I would like to remain in this death and sing hymns of praise unto You." If we remain in Christ's death in such a way, we shall have resurrection. The more resurrection we have, the more death we shall experience. Eventually, the out-resurrection, the outstanding resurrection, will be ours.

Many brothers and sisters have been baptized into Christ's death, but they do not remain in death. I can tell by the expression on their faces that they have come out of death, for it is obvious that they are not at rest. Everyone who remains in death is at rest....The reason there is conflict between a husband and wife is that they so often come out of death. By leaving death, they lose their rest....Only those who fully rest in death actually remain in Christ's death. These can say, "Praise the Lord that I have been baptized into His death. I am content to stay here." (*The Experience of Christ,* pp. 196-197)

Further Reading: The Experience of Christ, chs. 7, 14-21; *Life-study of Philippians,* msgs. 22, 53-54; *Words of Life,* chs. 5-6; *The Christian Life,* chs. 15-16

Enlightenment and inspiration: _____

_____

_____

_____

Morning Nourishment

John   Truly, truly, I say to you, Unless the grain of wheat
12:24-26 falls into the ground and dies, it abides alone; but
if it dies, it bears much fruit. He who loves his
soul-life loses it; and he who hates his soul-life in
this world shall keep it unto eternal life. If anyone
serves Me, let him follow Me; and where I am,
there also My servant will be. If anyone serves Me,
the Father will honor him.

32   And I, if I be lifted up from the earth, will draw all
men to Myself.

To be conformed to Christ's death is the real and practical
experience of Christ. To experience Christ to the uttermost is to
die and be conformed to His death. In the conformity to Christ's
death, we experience Christ in the release of His divine life. We
should not be content with mere outward increase. We must
care for how much life the new ones receive through our impartation, for how much life is infused into others through us. This
infusion of life depends not on our ability, strength, or teaching;
it depends on our being conformed to the death of Christ. We need
to be conformed to His death so that the divine life within us may
be released and imparted into others. Time will tell how much
life we have imparted into others. We may be able to stir up
people or excite them, but what counts is how much life is in
them after a number of years. (*The Experience of Christ,* p. 162)

Today's Reading

The Lord's death not only releases the divine life, but also
multiplies it. I regret that through the years I have not ade-
quately ministered life to you. Therefore, we are still short of
life. This shortage of life is probably due to the fact that I have
not died enough. Life comes out of death. The divine life is
within us, but how much this life is multiplied depends upon
how much death we undergo. The more death we experience,
the more life will be released from us. Only death can bring
about the multiplication of the divine life; power cannot do it.

Today's Christians devote their attention to power instead of to life. But only the death of Christ can multiply life.

Through the death of Christ, the Father is glorified (John 12:28; 13:31). Christ's death glorified the Father because it released the divine life. The release of the divine life from within Jesus was the glorification of God. Glory is God released and expressed. Hence, whenever the divine life within us is released, God is glorified. The unique way to glorify God is to die. The more we are conformed to the death of Christ, the more we glorify the Father. Many Christians are taught that the way to glorify God is to behave themselves. However, the more you behave yourself, the more you receive the glory. You do not give any glory to God. The only way to glorify God is to be conformed to the death of Christ. Then spontaneously the divine life within us will be released, and God the Father, the source of this life, will be glorified.

Another thing accomplished by the death of Christ is the saving of our soul (John 12:25). The only way to save our soul is to die. The more we die with Christ, the more we save our soul.

Through the death of Christ people are drawn to Christ. After telling Philip that He would die as a grain of wheat falling into the ground, the Lord said, "And I, if I be lifted up from the earth, will draw all men to Myself" (John 12:32). The words *lifted up* refer to the Lord's death on the cross. Through His death the Lord would draw men to Himself. The real attraction is in the dying. When we die the death of Christ and are conformed to His death, we shall be a magnet drawing people to Christ. The death of Christ on the cross has a lovable attraction. Such an attracting, the proper attraction, is not a matter of stirring up people emotionally. It is an attraction that comes through the release of life.…This is the crucified life with its attracting power. Every crucified person is a magnet. Wherever we are, we need to experience Christ in this way. (*The Experience of Christ*, pp. 163-164)

Further Reading: The Experience of Christ, ch. 18

Enlightenment and inspiration: _____

_____

_____

Morning Nourishment

Phil. If perhaps I may attain to the out-resurrection
3:11 from the dead.
Rev. Blessed and holy is he who has part in the first
20:6 resurrection; over these the second death has no
authority, but they will be priests of God and of
Christ and will reign with Him for a thousand years.
Heb. Women received their dead by resurrection; and
11:35 others were tortured *to death,* not accepting deliverance, in order that they might obtain a better
resurrection.

The out-resurrection from the dead denotes the outstanding
resurrection, the extra-resurrection, which will be a prize to the
overcoming saints. All believers who are dead in Christ will
participate in the resurrection from among the dead at the
Lord's coming back (1 Thes. 4:16; 1 Cor. 15:52). But the overcoming saints will enjoy an extra, outstanding portion of that
resurrection. This is the "better resurrection" mentioned in
Hebrews 11:35. The better resurrection is not only "the first
resurrection" (Rev. 20:4-6), "the resurrection of life" (John 5:28-
29), but also the out-resurrection, the resurrection in which the
Lord's overcomers will receive the reward of the kingdom, which
the apostle Paul sought after.

To arrive at the out-resurrection means that our entire
being has been gradually and continually resurrected. God
first resurrected our deadened spirit (Eph. 2:5-6). Then from
our spirit He proceeds to resurrect our soul (Rom. 8:6) and our
mortal body (Rom. 8:11), until our entire being—spirit, soul,
and body—is fully resurrected out of our old being by His
life and with His life. This is a process in life through which we
must pass and a race for us to run until we arrive at the
out-resurrection as the prize. Hence, the out-resurrection
should be the goal and destination of our Christian life. We can
only reach this goal by being conformed to the death of Christ,
by living a crucified life. In the death of Christ we are processed
in resurrection from the old creation to the new. (*Life-study of
Philippians,* pp. 188-189)

Today's Reading

Just as the goal is the out-resurrection, so the prize is also the out-resurrection. The goal is for us to gain, whereas the prize is for us to enjoy. We may reach the goal in this age, but we shall enjoy the prize in the coming age.

[Romans 8:11] indicates that we can attain to the out-resurrection in this age. Here Paul says that the Spirit of Him who raised Christ from among the dead will give life to that part of our being which is dying, our mortal bodies. We have seen that the Spirit is the reality of Christ's resurrection, the reality of the out-resurrection. The Spirit is dwelling in us to work the out-resurrection into our being in a real and practical way. Thus, Romans 8:11 indicates that we should attain to the out-resurrection in this age.

Revelation 20:6 refers to the prize in the coming age, the prize of the first resurrection: "Blessed and holy is he who has part in the first resurrection; over these the second death has no authority, but they will be priests of God and of Christ and will reign with Him for a thousand years." The Greek word rendered *first* is the same word used for the "best" robe given to the returned prodigal in Luke 15. The first resurrection is the best resurrection, the out-resurrection. If in this age we do not pursue a life which is absolutely out of the old creation and fully in God, we shall not have the prize for our enjoyment in the coming age. But if we obtain the out-resurrection today, it will become a prize to us in the next age. Then what is now our goal will become our prize when, during the millennium, we reign as co-kings with Christ. That will be the enjoyment of the out-resurrection as our prize. In Christ God has called us from above for this prize. This prize should be the goal we pursue and obtain in this age. (*Life-study of Philippians,* pp. 478-479)

Further Reading: Life-study of Philippians, msg. 22; *The Experience of Christ,* chs. 19-22

Enlightenment and inspiration: _____

_____

_____

Morning Nourishment

1 Thes. And the God of peace Himself sanctify you wholly,
5:23 and may your spirit and soul and body be preserved complete, without blame, at the coming of
our Lord Jesus Christ.

Eph. Even when we were dead in offenses, made us
2:5-6 alive together with Christ (by grace you have been
saved) and raised *us* up together with *Him*...

Rom. For the mind set on the flesh is death, but the mind
8:6 set on the spirit is life and peace.

Arriving at the out-resurrection is the result, the issue, of being conformed to Christ's death. To be conformed, molded, to the death of Christ means that we remain always in His death. If we remain in Christ's death, allowing ourselves to be molded into its likeness, the outcome will be that every part of our being will be gradually resurrected.

Our resurrection began with our regeneration. As sinners, we were all part of the old Adam. In every respect we were old. We were old in body, soul, and spirit. But when we believed in the Lord Jesus, something new entered into us. The Holy Spirit of God came in to regenerate us with the life of God. Thus, by regeneration, our old, deadened spirit was resurrected. The Bible says that when we were saved, we were made alive (Eph. 2:5). Before we were saved, we were dead in trespasses and sins (Eph. 2:1; Col. 2:13). But when we believed in the Lord Jesus, the Holy Spirit of God came in to enliven our deadened spirit with the divine life. At that time, part of our being, our spirit, was resurrected....God's goal is to resurrect our whole being. (*The Experience of Christ*, pp. 170-171)

Today's Reading

Suppose a certain brother is baptized, realizing that his natural life is being buried and that he has been enlivened by the divine life. From that time onward, he begins to walk toward the goal of having his entire being brought into resur-rection. He loves the Lord and prays to the Lord with the

expectation that eventually every part of him will be resurrected. He begins to have the excellency of the knowledge of
Christ and, one by one, he begins to count things loss so that
he may gain Christ and be found in Him in a condition of not
having his own righteousness out from the law, but of having
God Himself lived out of him as his righteousness. He also
begins to experientially know Christ, the power of His resurrection, and the fellowship of His sufferings. Gradually, he also
begins to be conformed to the death of Christ. As he seeks the
Lord and experiences Him, he spontaneously realizes, item by
item, the things in him that have been terminated. For example, one day he may come to see that his love for his wife should
not be a natural love. Thus, he may pray, "Lord, I confess that
my love for my wife has been a natural love. Grant me the grace
to live a crucified life with my wife." This is to be conformed to
Christ's death in the particular matter of loving his wife.
Several days later he may realize that even his contact with
the saints has been too natural. He has cared for the saints
and tried to shepherd them, but even in his shepherding he
has been too natural. Therefore, he prays and confesses this
matter to the Lord, asking Him for the grace to no longer
shepherd the saints according to his natural life. He may pray,
"Lord, I want to be conformed to Your death. Like You, I want
to live a crucified life. When You were on earth, You did not love
people or care for them according to the natural life. Everything You did was in resurrection. Lord, grant me the grace
that from now on I will not shepherd Your saints in my natural
life, but in You." Through this experience, he becomes conformed to the death of Christ in this matter also. Item by item,
he is conformed to Christ's death. The more he is conformed to
Christ's death in this way, the more his being is resurrected.
In loving his wife and in shepherding the saints, he is resurrected. (*The Experience of Christ*, pp. 172-173)

Further Reading: The Experience of Christ, chs. 19-22; *Life-
study of Philippians*, msgs. 22, 54-55

Enlightenment and inspiration: _____

_____

_____

Morning Nourishment

John 14:20 In that day you will know that I *am* in My
            Father, and you in Me, and I in you.
 Phil. 1:21 For to me, to live is Christ...
John 11:25 Jesus said to her, I am the resurrection and the
            life; he who believes into Me, even if he should
            die, shall live.

We have seen that this out-resurrection is actually the dear,
precious, excellent person of Christ, the very One who, through
crucifixion and resurrection, has passed out of the old creation
and has entered into God. This wonderful One is far more
excellent than the angels. Angels still belong to the old creation. They have not experienced crucifixion or resurrection. But
after Christ was crucified and buried, He was resurrected out
of the old creation and into God. Have you ever heard such a
description of the Lord Jesus? Hallelujah, Christ Himself is the
reality of the out-resurrection! Now we must pursue a life
which is this wonderful person of Christ. With Paul we should
be able to say, "To me, to live is Christ" (Phil. 1:21). Paul could
also testify that he had been crucified with Christ and that
Christ lived in him (Gal. 2:20). The very Christ who lived in
Paul is the One who, in His own person, is the out-resurrection.
(*Life-study of Philippians,* pp. 482-483)

Today's Reading

In 1:21 Paul says, "To me, to live is Christ." This Christ was
his goal. Hence, for Paul to live was the goal—Christ as the out-
resurrection. Furthermore, for us to live should also be the
out-resurrection, for the very Christ whom we should live is
Himself the out-resurrection. This means that day by day we
should live the out-resurrection. For example, suppose a certain brother loves his wife very much. He needs to ask himself
whether this love is natural or in resurrection. Even non-
Christian husbands may love their wives in a natural way. If
a brother loves his wife in resurrection, his love will be out of
the old creation and in God. This shows that to live Christ is

to live the out-resurrection, to live a life absolutely out of the old creation and in God.

When I was young, I wondered why it seemed difficult for Paul to reach the goal. I thought that the persecutions he suffered made this difficult. It seemed to me opposition from others hindered him in running the Christian race. Years later, through experience I came to see that it is easier for me to overcome persecutions than to love my wife in the out-resurrection and not according to the natural life. I have been in Christ for more than fifty years. During all this time I have been a zealous Christian. Having encountered many hindrances in the Christian race, I have learned that the greatest hindrance is the natural life with its thoughts and habits. The natural life frustrates in running the race toward the goal.

Have you ever asked yourself how much of your daily conversation is natural and how much is in the out-resurrection? Although you may not speak in an evil, slanderous way, your talk may be natural. You may speak many positive things, but your words may be spoken in a natural way, not in resurrection. It is easy to improve our character, behavior, ethics, or morality, but it is extremely difficult to live in resurrection.

Paul knew from experience that it is not easy to live a life which is wholly out of the old creation and in God. In 1:21 he could declare, "To me, to live is Christ." But in chapter one we simply have the declaration, not the explanation or definition. In chapter three we see that to live Christ is to live the out-resurrection and that this should be our goal. Our deeds and words must be in resurrection. If a certain deed is not in resurrection, we should not do it. If a certain word is not in resurrection, we should not say it. The question is not whether a particular thing is right or wrong, but whether or not it is in resurrection. Even our love needs to be in resurrection. (*Life-study of Philippians*, pp. 476-477)

Further Reading: The Experience of Christ, chs. 19-22; Life-study of Philippians, msgs. 22, 54-55

Enlightenment and inspiration: _____

_____

_____

Hymns, #482

1   I am crucified with Christ,
And the cross hath set me free;
I have ris'n again with Christ,
And He lives and reigns in me.

     Oh! it is so sweet to die with Christ,
To the world, and self, and sin;
Oh! it is so sweet to live with Christ,
As He lives and reigns within.

2   Mystery hid from ancient ages!
But at length to faith made plain:
Christ in me the Hope of Glory,
Tell it o'er and o'er again.

3   This the secret nature hideth,
Harvest grows from buried grain;
A poor tree with better grafted,
Richer, sweeter life doth gain.

4   This the secret of the holy,
Not our holiness, but Him;
O Lord! empty us and fill us,
With Thy fulness to the brim.

5   This the balm for pain and sickness,
Just to all our strength to die,
And to find His life and fulness,
All our being's need supply.

6   This the story of the Master,
Thru the Cross, He reached the Throne,
And like Him our path to glory,
Ever leads through death alone.

Composition for prophecy with main point and sub-points: _____

_____

_____

_____

_____

_____

_____

_____

_____

_____

_____

_____

_____

_____

_____

_____

_____

_____

_____

_____

_____

_____

_____

_____

_____

_____

_____

_____

_____

_____

_____

_____

Taking Christ as Our Virtues

Scripture Reading: Phil. 4:5-9

Day 1
I. The virtues of Christ for our experience in Philippians 4:5-9 are the expression of a life that lives Christ (1:19-21a; 2:5-13; 3:8-10):

A. Paul considers forbearance and the lack of anxiety as the first two aspects of the expression of a life that lives Christ.

B. Anxiety, coming from Satan, is the sum total of human life and disturbs the believers' life of living Christ; forbearance, coming from God, is the sum total of a life that lives Christ; the two are opposites.

Day 2
II. "Let your forbearance be known to all men. The Lord is near" (4:5):

A. Forbearance is reasonableness, considerateness, and consideration in dealing with others, without being strict in claiming one's legal rights; forbearance means that we are easily satisfied, even with less than our due:

1. According to Christian experience, forbearance is all-inclusive, for it includes all Christian virtues:

    a. Forbearance includes love, patience, kindness, humility, compassion, considerateness, and submissiveness, a willingness to yield; if we have such an all-inclusive virtue, we shall also have righteousness and holiness.

    b. Forbearance also includes self-control, moderation, gentleness, understanding, sympathy, wisdom, mercy, peacefulness, looking to the Lord, and even the virtue of admitting that the Lord is sovereign in all things.

2. A forbearing person is one who always fits in, whose behavior is always suitable (cf. 2 Cor. 6:1a; 10:1; Phil. 1:19; Isa. 11:2):

    a. If we are forbearing, we shall have the wisdom and the ability to supply others with what they need; we shall also have the full knowledge of what to say to them and when to say it (50:4-5; Col. 1:28).

    b. To be forbearing is to consider how others will be affected by what we do or say (2 Chron. 1:10).

Day 3

  3. As an all-inclusive virtue, forbearance is Christ Himself; since Christ is forbearance, for Paul to live was forbearance (Phil. 1:21a):

    a. To let our forbearance be known to all men is to let the Christ whom we live and magnify, whom we take as our pattern and pursue as our goal, be known to all men.

    b. Only the Lord Jesus lived a life full of forbearance, and only Christ can be our perfect forbearance today.

    c. To make known our forbearance is to live a life which expresses Christ as the totality of all human virtues.

B. Immediately after speaking about forbearance, Paul said that the Lord is near:

  1. With respect to space, the Lord is near us, ready to help; with regard to time, the Lord is at hand, coming soon (cf. Rom. 10:8-13).

  2. The Lord's being near refers primarily to His presence with us (Matt. 1:23).

Day 4

III. "In nothing be anxious, but in everything, by prayer and petition with thanksgiving, let your requests be made known to God; and the peace of God, which surpasses every man's understanding, will guard your hearts and your thoughts in Christ Jesus" (Phil. 4:6-7):

A. The words *in everything* refer to the many different things which happen to us day by day.

B. Prayer is general, having worship and fellowship as its essence; petition is special, being for particular needs; both our prayer and our petition should be accompanied by our giving thanks to the Lord.

C. *To God* denotes motion toward, in the sense of a living union and communion, implying fellowship; hence, the sense of *to God* here is *in the fellowship with God*.

D. The result of practicing fellowship with God in prayer is that we enjoy the peace of God; the peace of God is actually God as peace (v. 9) infused into us through our fellowship with Him by prayer, as the counterpoise to troubles and the antidote to anxiety (John 16:33).

Day 5

E. The God of peace patrols before our hearts and thoughts in Christ, keeping us calm and tranquil.

F. If we would have a life free of anxiety, we need to realize that all our circumstances, good or bad, have been assigned to us by God in order to serve us in fulfilling our destiny to gain Christ, live Christ, and magnify Christ (Rom. 8:28-30; Matt. 10:29-30; 2 Cor. 4:15-18).

Day 6

IV. **"Finally, brothers, what things are true, what things are dignified, what things are righteous, what things are pure, what things are lovely, what things are well spoken of, if there is any virtue and if any praise, take account of these things" (Phil. 4:8):**

A. These virtues are the expressions of God's attributes lived out from within the pursuers of Christ, who is the embodiment of God.

B. These virtues are six governing aspects of a life that lives Christ:

1. A life that lives Christ is true—ethically truthful, without any pretense or falsehood.

2. A life that lives Christ is dignified—honorable, noble, grave, solid, weighty, and worthy of reverence (1 Tim. 3:8, 11; Titus 2:2; cf. Rom. 9:21).

3. A life that lives Christ is righteous—right before God and man.

4. A life that lives Christ is pure—single in intention and action, without any mixture (Matt. 5:8).

5. A life that lives Christ is lovely—lovable, agreeable, and endearing.

6. A life that lives Christ is well spoken of—renowned, of good repute, attractive, winning, and gracious.

C. Virtue and praise are a summing up of the six foregoing items, in all of which are some virtue or excellence and something worthy of praise (v. 16).

D. To be a proper human being is to express God through His divine attributes in our human virtues, to have a human life filled with Christ as the reality of the attributes of God (cf. Gen. 1:26).

Morning Nourishment

Phil. 4:5-6 Let your forbearance be known to all men. The Lord is near. In nothing be anxious...

1:21 For to me, to live is Christ...

2:5 Let this mind be in you, which was also in Christ Jesus.

3:8 But moreover I also count all things to be loss on account of the excellency of the knowledge of Christ Jesus my Lord, on account of whom I have suffered the loss of all things and count *them* as refuse that I may gain Christ.

I have come to realize that...anxiety is the totality of human life...[and] forbearance is the totality of the Christian life. This is the reason Paul uses the words *forbearance* and *anxiety* together in charging the saints. Positively, we should make known our forbearance. All those who come in contact with us should know our forbearance. Negatively, we need to have a life without anxiety.

To be a proper human being we need to be Christians, and to be normal Christians we need to have the church life. However, if we are to have the proper and genuine church life, we need a life full of forbearance but without anxiety. To have such a life is to live Christ. (*Life-study of Philippians,* p. 528)

Today's Reading

Philippians 4 is a word of conclusion. As he was composing this concluding word, Paul was still motivated by those factors which caused him to write the first three chapters. He was still considering such matters as thinking the same thing by pursuing Christ and rejoicing in the Lord in order to enjoy the riches of Christ. In the first three chapters of Philippians, Paul refers to the inner reality of the experience of Christ. But prior to chapter four, he does not give any illustrations of the outer expression of this reality. If we enjoy Christ and experience Him, we shall have a certain inner reality. Such an inward reality invariably issues in an outward expression. In 4:5-9 we find a full expression of this inward reality, a full expression of a life that lives Christ.

In 1:21 Paul declares, "To me, to live is Christ." This statement is a testimony of Paul's inner reality. But what is the real expression of a life that lives Christ? This expression is found in the virtues listed in 4:5-9. In the same principle, in chapter two Paul sets forth Christ as our pattern. Suppose we take the crucified and exalted Christ as our pattern. What will be the expression of a life which lives according to this pattern? The expression is in 4:5-9. The same is true with respect to Paul's word in chapter three concerning counting all things loss, even refuse, in order to gain Christ. What kind of expression will there be in a person's life if that one condemns philosophy, rejects culture, and renounces religion, counting them as refuse in order to gain Christ? What kind of life will such a person live, and what will be the practical expression of this life? Once again we would point out that the expression is seen in 4:5-9.

The basic factor within Paul motivating him to write this concluding word was the need to show the expression of a life that lives Christ, that takes Christ as the pattern, that counts all religious, philosophical, and cultural things as refuse, and that enjoys Christ as everything. With this as his motivation, Paul composed chapter four as a concluding word to this Epistle.

This portion of Philippians presents the expression of a life that lives Christ—a life that takes Christ as the pattern and counts all things refuse in order to gain more of Christ.

The first aspect of the expression of a life that lives Christ is forbearance. Philippians 4:5 says, "Let your forbearance be known to all men."...A second aspect is the absence of anxiety. In a life that lives Christ there will be forbearance, but no anxiety, no worry. Paul considers forbearance and the lack of anxiety as the first two aspects of the expression of a life that lives Christ. (*Life-study of Philippians*, pp. 225-227)

Further Reading: Life-study of Philippians, msgs. 27, 56-57, 60-61; *The Experience and Growth in Life*, msgs. 13, 15

Enlightenment and inspiration: _____

_____

_____

Morning Nourishment

Phil. Let your forbearance be known to all men. The
4:5 Lord is near.

2 Cor. But I myself, Paul, entreat you through the meek-
10:1 ness and gentleness of Christ, who *(as you say)* in
person am base among you, but while absent am
bold toward you.

2 Chron. Now give me wisdom and knowledge, that I may
1:10 go out and come in before this people...

In his *Word Studies* Wuest points out that the Greek word
rendered *forbearance* not only means satisfied with less than
our due, but also means sweet reasonableness. The word
includes self-control, patience, moderation, kindness, and gentleness. Furthermore, according to Christian experience, forbearance is all-inclusive, for it includes all Christian virtues.
This means that if we fail to exercise forbearance, we fail to
exercise any Christian virtue. If a brother's wife serves him a
cold drink contrary to his preference and he complains about
it, then at that time he does not exhibit any Christian virtue.
But if by the grace of Christ he is satisfied with less than his
due and exercises forbearance toward his wife, not criticizing
her or condemning her, he will show in his forbearance an
all-inclusive Christian virtue. His forbearance will include
patience, humility, self-control, looking to the Lord, and even
the virtue of admitting that the Lord is sovereign in all things.

The reason we sometimes behave in an unseemly manner
is that we lack forbearance. Negative attitudes and unkind
words also come from a shortage of forbearance....If we do not
have forbearance, we shall not have peace. If we do not show
forbearance toward the members of our family, there will be no
peace in our family life. Peace comes out of forbearance. (*Life-
study of Philippians*, p. 494)

Today's Reading

In every chapter of Philippians Christ is revealed. However, in chapter four a particular term—forbearance—is used to denote Christ in our experience. Do not think that chapter four of Philippians is on a lower level than chapters one, two, and three. No, in chapter four we have Christ experienced by us and expressed through us as forbearance. We may say that the central focus of our Christian life is Christ. I certainly agree with such a statement. But from the standpoint of our practical Christian experience, the focus of the Christian life is forbearance. Forbearance is an all-inclusive Christian virtue. It includes love, patience, kindness, humility, compassion, considerateness, and submissiveness, a willingness to yield. If we have such an all-inclusive virtue, we shall also have righteousness and holiness.

A forbearing person is one who always fits in, one whose behavior is always suitable. Certain saints are good, but they do not fit in. They may move from place to place, but no matter where they may go, they are not happy. The reason these saints do not fit in is that they are not forbearing. A forbearing person is one who always fits in, whose behavior is always suitable, no matter what the circumstances or environment may be.

Forbearance also includes peacefulness, mildness, and gentleness. If you are reasonable, considerate, and able to fit in, you will no doubt be gentle, kind, mild, and peaceful. You will also be meek and moderate, full of compassion for others. As we pointed out in the previous message, the opposite of forbearance is being just in a very exacting way. A person who lacks forbearance will be exacting and demanding of others. But to be forbearing means that we are satisfied with less than our due. Alford says that the Greek word for forbearance means to not be strict with respect to legal rights. For example, a certain thing may be ours, but we do not claim it according to strict, legal right. This is forbearance. (*Life-study of Philippians,* pp. 503-504)

Further Reading: Life-study of Philippians, msgs. 56-59; *The Experience and Growth in Life,* msg. 13

Enlightenment and inspiration: _____

_____

_____

_____

Morning Nourishment

Phil. 1:21 For to me, to live is Christ...

Matt. 1:23 "Behold, the virgin shall be with child and shall bear a son, and they shall call His name Emmanuel" (which is translated, God with us).

Rom. 10:8 But what does it say? "The word is near you, in your mouth and in your heart," that is, the word of the faith which we proclaim.

Paul realized that forbearance is an all-inclusive virtue. This is the reason he says, "Let your forbearance be known to all men" [Phil. 4:5]. This forbearance is actually Christ Himself. In 1:21 Paul says, "To me, to live is Christ." Since Christ is forbearance, for Paul to live was forbearance. Paul's earnest expectation was that Christ would be magnified in him, whether through life or through death. For Paul to magnify Christ was for him to make known his forbearance. Thus, for Christ to be magnified in us is equal to making our forbearance known to all men. The reason for this is that forbearance is Christ experienced by us in a practical way. We may speak of living Christ and testify that for us to live is Christ. However, day by day in our life at home what we need is forbearance. If we have forbearance, then in our experience we truly have Christ. If a brother's wife offends him, what he needs to make known to her is Christ as his forbearance. (*Life-study of Philippians,* p. 495)

Today's Reading

It is very difficult to be a good husband or wife. The key to being a good husband or wife is forbearance. To repeat, forbearance includes much more than gentleness or humility. As an all-inclusive Christian virtue, forbearance is Christ Himself. In both the family life and in the church life, we need to live Christ by living a life of forbearance.

The more we consider the significance of forbearance, the more we can appreciate why Paul spoke of it in 4:5. Our failures and defeats in the Christian life come because we are short of forbearance. All the saints, young and old alike, have a tendency to neglect forbearance. If we would live Christ, we must be satisfied with less than our due. We should not make exacting demands on others.

The Lord Jesus lived a life of forbearance when He was on earth. In one sense, He was very strict, but in another sense He was very tolerant. For example, although He prayed a great deal, He did not make demands of His disciples concerning prayer or condemn them because they did not pray enough.

Immediately after speaking about forbearance, Paul goes on to say, "The Lord is near."...I do not oppose the understanding that this refers to the nearness of the Lord's coming. Nevertheless, according to experience, not according to doctrine, I would say that this word refers to the Lord's presence with us today. It also strengthens Paul's exhortation that we make our forbearance known to all men. Because the Lord is near, we have no excuse for not making known our forbearance. Often we fail to exercise forbearance because we forget that the Lord is near. We do not even remember that He is actually within us. When a brother's wife serves him a cold drink instead of a hot one, will he care for the drink or for the Lord? If he cares about the drink instead of the Lord, then in his experience only the drink will be at hand, for the Lord will be far away. Because we do not realize that the Lord is near, we do not exercise forbearance. Instead, we are strict in dealing with others and make exacting demands of them without considering their situation. The more we realize the nearness of the Lord, the more satisfied we shall be and the more we shall be considerate of others and sweetly reasonable regarding their situation. If we realize that the Lord is near, we shall turn from the old creation to the new creation, to the out-resurrection, which is expressed as forbearance. (*Life-study of Philippians,* pp. 495-496)

Further Reading: Life-study of Philippians, msgs. 56-61; *The Experience and Growth in Life,* msg. 13*

Enlightenment and inspiration: _____

_____

_____

Morning Nourishment

Phil. **In nothing be anxious, but in everything, by prayer**
4:6-7 **and petition with thanksgiving, let your requests be**
made known to God; and the peace of God, which
surpasses every *man's* understanding, will guard
your hearts and your thoughts in Christ Jesus.

9 **The things which you have also learned and re-**
ceived and heard and seen in me, practice these
things; and the God of peace will be with you.

John **These things I have spoken to you that in Me you**
16:33 **may have peace. In the world you have affliction,**
but take courage; I have overcome the world.

In Philippians 4:5 we are encouraged to express Christ as
our forbearance. But the thing which opposes forbearance is
our anxiety (v. 6). Anxiety is versus forbearance. If you live
Christ, the character of your expression will be forbearance.
But if you are a person who is full of anxiety, the character of
your expression will be worry. Our anxiety can be turned into
forbearance by bringing every need, every request, to God (v. 6)
and by conversing with Him. To converse implies a kind of
traffic back and forth. Every morning, regardless of how busy
we are, we need such traffic between us and God. This kind of
traffic brings in the divine dispensing, reduces our anxiety, and
builds up our forbearance. It is by this traffic, the fellowship
between us and God, that we enjoy the divine dispensing. (*The
Experience and Growth in Life*, p. 99)

Today's Reading

Prayer [in verse 6] is general with the essence of worship
and fellowship; petition is special for particular needs. Both
our prayer and petition should be accompanied by thanksgiving to the Lord. The English preposition *to* in the phrase *to God*
is the Greek preposition *pros*. This preposition...denotes motion towards, in the sense of a living union and communion;
thus, it implies fellowship. Hence, the meaning of *to God* here
is *in fellowship with God*. John 1:1 uses the preposition *pros*

in the phrase *the Word was with* (pros) *God.* Such a word conveys the thought of traffic, something going back and forth. It denotes motion toward some object which produces a transaction in the sense of a living union. Based upon this union, there is communion which is a communication or fellowship.

Whenever we pray, making our petition in the proper way, there should be some traffic between us and God. Something from us should move toward God, causing God to respond to us. This moving back and forth is fellowship. This is the proper meaning of the word *fellowship.* Fellowship is actually the dispensing of God for man to receive. The fellowship we have with God is, on God's side, His dispensing and, on our side, our receiving. He dispenses, and we receive. The more fellowship we have, the more we receive of God through His dispensing.

The practical mingling of divinity with humanity is carried out by the traffic described in verse 6. We must come to God by prayer often. This is the reason the New Testament tells us to pray unceasingly (1 Thes. 5:17). To pray is to breathe God in. To pray is also to have a traffic between us and God. This two-way traffic is our union, communion, and fellowship. The current of electricity is its traffic, communion, or fellowship. Without the current of electricity, we could not enjoy the operation of electrical appliances such as lights. It is the same between us and God. Within us there must always be traffic, a current, between us and God. When we stop praying, the traffic stops. Then whatever we do is something in ourselves without God. When we pray unceasingly, keeping ourselves in the current, the fellowship, the communion, the traffic, we enjoy the mingling of divinity with humanity. Then as we exercise our love, we express God's love. Our love is our virtue mingled with God's love, God's attribute. We then become a mingled entity, a God-man, having divinity mingled with our humanity. (*The Experience and Growth in Life,* pp. 97-98, 104-105)

Further Reading: The Experience and Growth in Life, msg. 15; *Life-study of Philippians,* msg. 27

Enlightenment and inspiration: _____

_____

_____

Morning Nourishment

Rom. And we know that all things work together for
8:28 good to those who love God, to those who are
called according to *His* purpose.

Matt. Are not two sparrows sold for an assarion? And
10:29 not one of them will fall to the earth apart from
your Father.

2 Cor. Therefore we do not lose heart; but though our
4:16-17 outer man is decaying, yet our inner *man* is being
renewed day by day. For our momentary lightness
of affliction works out for us, more and more
surpassingly, an eternal weight of glory.

Whether or not we can exercise forbearance in difficult
situations depends on the kind of realization and practice we
have. If we realize that a particular situation is of the Lord,
that it is needed to perfect us, and then thank Him for it, we
shall not be anxious or threatened. We shall be able to say,
"Lord, I thank You for this. I am not threatened by this thing,
because I know that I am one with You and that everything
which comes to me is Your assignment. Lord, I also know that
You allow this thing to remain that it may help You to fulfill
Your purpose and to perfect me." If we realize that everything
is the Lord's assignment and if we accept His will and thank
Him for it, we shall be able to say with Paul, "Therefore we do
not lose heart; but though our outer man is decaying, yet our
inner man is being renewed day by day. For our momentary
lightness of affliction works out for us, more and more surpassingly, an eternal weight of glory" (2 Cor. 4:16-17). Then we shall
not have any anxiety. (*Life-study of Philippians*, pp. 547-548)

Today's Reading

The first prerequisite to having no anxiety is to have the
full assurance that all the sufferings we experience are God's
assignment. What need is there to worry about things? God
has assigned them to us. He knows what we need....But
sometimes He sends us hardships and sufferings to serve in

fulfilling our destiny to magnify Christ. We can be freed from worry not because God has promised us a life without suffering, but because we know that all our circumstances come to us as God's assignment. Faul did not care about life or death. He cared only that Christ would be magnified in him. He realized that every circumstance was for his good. This is the way to have no anxiety.

Why do certain saints worry about losing money? Simply because their desire is to have more money. Why are others anxious about their health? They are anxious because they are afraid to die. If we are ill, we need to declare, "Satan, what can you do to me? I am not worried about death. Death does not make me anxious. Rather, the possibility of dying gives me another opportunity to magnify Christ." Instead of fearing poverty, illness, or death, we should welcome them if God sends them to us. Then we shall have no anxiety, for we shall know that every circumstance is an assignment from our Father. This does not mean, however, that we should seek suffering for its own sake. We should not do things that will cause us to suffer. Those who are in business should seek to make money, and those who are employees should try to get a promotion. But if we lose money or even lose our job, we need not be anxious. Such a loss comes from God's assignment, and we need not be anxious about it.

If we would not have any anxiety, we must recognize that all afflictions, sufferings, calamities, disasters, and catastrophies are assigned by God. We also must be one with the Lord in our experience. Yes, we may realize the necessity of passing through suffering and affliction. But if we would be free from anxiety, we need something more than this realization. We must also be one with the Lord. Otherwise, eventually our circumstances or the things which happen to us will cause anxiety, and we shall not be satisfied with anything or anyone. (*Life-study of Philippians,* pp. 531-532, 543)

Further Reading: Life-study of Philippians, msgs. 60-62

Enlightenment and inspiration: _____

_____

_____

Morning Nourishment

Phil. Finally, brothers, what things are true, what
4:8 things are dignified, what things are righteous,
what things are pure, what things are lovely, what
things are well spoken of, if there is any virtue and
if any praise, take account of these things.

Gen. And God said, Let Us make man in Our image,
1:26 according to Our likeness; and let them have
dominion...

Matt. In the same way, let your light shine before men,
5:16 so that they may see your good works and glorify
your Father who is in the heavens.

In Philippians 4:8 Paul presents six items which express
the life that lives Christ....These items form three pairs. The
first pair is *true* and *dignified.* The second pair is *righteous*
and *pure.* The third pair is *lovely* and *well spoken of.* Verse 8
concludes with two matters: "If there is any virtue and if any
praise, take account of these things." All of these items are
very human. Some saints are very desirous to live Christ but
in a way that is not very human. These six items with two
concluding matters describe how human we should be in
living Christ. We should be true, without any pretense or
falsehood. We also should be dignified, which means that we
are people who invite honor, regard, and respect from others.
As those who live Christ, we should be righteous before God
and men, and we should also be pure. To be righteous is to be
right without; to be pure is to be single in our intention and
motive within. We must be right without and pure within. We
should also be lovely and well spoken of. To be lovely is to be
lovable, agreeable, and endearing. To be well spoken of is to
be of good repute, renowned, attractive, winning, gracious,
and even charming. (*The Experience and Growth in Life,*
pp. 88-89)

Today's Reading

Although all of the foregoing items are human virtues, we

must realize that these human virtues are the vessel created by God to contain His attributes. A glove is made in the image and likeness of a hand as a container for the hand with its fingers. Without the hand with its fingers, the glove is empty. In the same way, we were made in God's image and likeness. He is the true God, and He has made us in a way that we can contain Him. God is true, and man can also be true. God is honorable, and God also made man with honor. The items in Philippians 4:8 are not only the virtues of man, but also the attributes of God.

We are vessels made to contain God for His expression, so we have the outward form of these attributes but not their reality. When we live Christ, who is the embodiment of God with all the attributes of God, He fills up all of our empty virtues. God's attributes then become our virtues. Thus, living Christ makes us very human. We should not only be spiritual and heavenly but also be true, dignified, righteous, pure, lovely, and well spoken of. These human virtues with the divine attributes are the detailed expression of the Christ we live and magnify. If we are not lovely and honorable, we are not expressing Christ. If we do not live an honorable life, we are not living Christ. If we live and magnify Christ, we will surely live an honorable life.

To be a person full of Christ as the proper virtues is to experience God's salvation. In Philippians 1 salvation is to live Christ and magnify Christ in any circumstance. Chapter two shows us that this salvation is to reflect Christ by holding forth the word of life. In chapter three salvation is the righteousness of God, who is God Himself embodied in Christ. Then in chapter four, there is the life that is true, dignified, righteous, pure, lovely, well-spoken of, and full of virtue and praise. (*The Experience and Growth in Life*, pp. 89, 93)

Further Reading: The Experience and Growth in Life, msgs. 13-15, 18; *Life-study of Philippians,* msg. 28

Enlightenment and inspiration: _____

_____

_____

_____

Hymns, #399

1   Changed into His likeness!
      This my heart's desire!
   May the Lord fulfill it,
      All my soul inspire.

2   Changed into His likeness!
      He the Spirit is!
   If the Spirit governs,
      He'll fulfill my wish.

3   As a glass, beholding
      With uncovered face,
   I can see His glory
      And reflect His grace.

4   O that no more covering
      May the Lord obscure,
   That I may reflect Him
      With a heart made pure.

5   Gazing on His glory,
      Face to face to see;
   Constantly beholding,
      Ever would I be.

6   Changed into His likeness!
      This my heart's one quest!
   From my heart reflected,
      He will be expressed.

7   Changed into His likeness
      And reflecting more
   Glory unto glory,
      Boundless evermore.

Composition for prophecy with main point and sub-points: _____

_____

_____

_____

_____

_____

_____

_____

_____

_____

_____

_____

_____

_____

_____

_____

_____

_____

_____

_____

_____

_____

_____

_____

_____

_____

_____

_____

_____

_____

_____

Taking Christ as Our Secret
and as Our Power

Scripture Reading: Phil. 4:11-13

Day 1
I. The subject of the book of Philippians is the experience of Christ in every kind of circumstance (1:19-21a; 2:5; 3:9-10; 4:11-13).

II. In Philippians 4 Christ is the secret and the power for us to enjoy; we know the secret, and we have the power (vv. 12-13).

III. Paul had learned the secret of sufficiency, of satisfaction, of contentment; this secret is actually Christ Himself (vv. 11-12):

A. In any environment and in any matter, Paul, who experienced Christ richly and abundantly, learned the secret to be content and to rejoice always (v. 4).

B. According to the book of Philippians as a whole, the secret Paul learned was simply Christ; Paul took Christ as the secret to experience Christ, being content and rejoicing in any situation and in any matter because of Christ.

Day 2
C. Paul had not only learned a secret; he had been initiated and had learned certain basic principles (v. 12):

1. Paul had been initiated both into the proper Christian life and into the proper church life.

2. After Paul was converted to Christ, he was initiated into Christ and into the Body of Christ (Acts 9:3-19, 25-28; 22:6-21; 13:1-4):

a. He was initiated into the basic principles of Christ and the church.

b. He learned the secret of how to take Christ as life (Col. 3:4), how to live Christ (Phil. 1:21a), how to magnify Christ (v. 20), how to gain Christ (3:8, 12), and how to have the church life (1:8, 19; 2:1-4, 19-20; 4:1-3).

D. When we are saved and come into the church, the Body of Christ, we need to be initiated by learning certain basic principles (1 Tim. 3:15-16):

1. We are initiated in Christ, with Christ, and by Christ; because Christ is our secret, we know how to face any kind of situation.

2. Because the church has a mysterious aspect, we need to be initiated by learning certain basic principles (Eph. 3:3, 9; 5:32).

3. The secret of the Body is to take Christ as our life, to live Christ, to pursue Christ, to gain Christ, to magnify Christ, and to express Christ; these are the basic principles of the church, the Body of Christ (Rom. 12:4-5).

Day 3

E. *In everything* refers to a particular time when we experience a certain thing of the Lord; *in all things* refers to a broad range of experiences over time (Phil. 4:12):

1. Paul could say that both on a particular occasion and on all occasions, both at a certain time and throughout the course of his life, he had learned the secret.

2. Paul experienced Christ moment by moment:

   a. He experienced Christ in particular things at particular times.

   b. He experienced Christ in all things and at all times.

Day 4

IV. In verse 13 we have a basic principle related to Paul's secret of sufficiency in Christ: "I am able to do all things in Him who empowers me":

A. The secret in Philippians 4 is to do all things in Christ (John 15:4a, 5):

1. Whatever we do should be done in Christ, not in ourselves; this is the secret Paul learned and the secret we need to learn today.

2. It is sufficient for us to be in Christ, for He is all-inclusive.

3. The way to experience Christ is to do everything in Him.

   4. If we do all things in Christ, we shall experience Christ, enjoy Christ, and accumulate Christ; this is the way to become rich in Christ and to have many rich experiences of Christ (Eph. 3:8).
   5. The issue of practicing the secret of being in Christ is that for us to live is Christ; because we do all things in Christ, we live Christ (Phil. 1:21a).

Day 5   B. Paul's word in 4:13 is an all-inclusive and concluding word on his experience of Christ:
   1. Paul was a person in Christ, and he desired to be found by others in Christ (2 Cor. 12:2a; Phil. 3:9).
   2. In 4:13 he declared that, being in Christ, he could do all things in Him, the very Christ who empowered him; this was his secret.
   3. As a person in Christ, Paul experienced Christ and applied Him in all circumstances (vv. 11-12):
      a. Paul applied the Christ in whom he could be found (3:9).
      b. This Christ is real, living, near, available, and prevailing (4:5b).

Day 6   C. To be empowered is to be made dynamic inwardly (v. 13):
   1. Christ dwells in us, and He empowers us, makes us dynamic, from within, not from without (Col. 1:27).
   2. By such an inward empowering Paul could do all things in Christ.

   D. Paul's word about Christ as the empowering One specifically applies to Christ's empowering us to live Him as our human virtues and thereby to magnify Him in His unlimited greatness (Phil. 4:8-13):
   1. The application of verse 13 is limited by the context of verses 8 through 13.

    2. By the empowering of Christ we can live a contented life and be true, dignified, righteous, pure, lovely, and well spoken of (vv. 11-12, 8).

    3. To live a life of these virtues is much more difficult than doing a Christian work.

    4. We are persons in Christ, who empowers us to live out every kind of virtue; this is to live Christ and to magnify Him in His virtues (1:20-21a).

E. If we would experience Christ as the empowering One, we need to let Him live in us (Gal. 2:20), be formed in us (4:19), make His home in us (Eph. 3:17a), and be magnified in us (Phil. 1:20):

    1. If we fail to do these things, Christ will not have the way to empower us.

    2. When Christ lives in us, is formed in us, makes His home in us, and is magnified in us, the way is prepared for Him to empower us; then, empowered by the indwelling Christ, we shall be able to do all the things spoken of in 4:8-12.

Morning Nourishment

Phil. 4:4 Rejoice in the Lord always; again I will say, rejoice.
11-13 Not that I speak according to lack, for I have learned, in whatever circumstances I am, to be content. I know also how to be abased, and I know how to abound; in everything and in all things I have learned the secret both to be filled and to hunger, both to abound and to lack. I am able to do all things in Him who empowers me.

[Now] we shall consider Paul's secret of sufficiency in Christ. Paul had learned the secret of sufficiency, of satisfaction, of contentment. This secret is actually Christ Himself. In Philippians 1, Christ is the life for us to live; in chapter two, Christ is the pattern for us to follow; and in chapter three, Christ is the goal and the prize for us to pursue. Now in chapter four, Christ is the secret and also the power for us to enjoy. In doing many things we must first know the secret and also have the power, the strength, the energy, to accomplish those things.

In teaching people to do things, even insignificant things, we mainly teach them the secret. This is true, for example, in teaching someone the art of barbecuing meat. If a person does not learn the secret of barbecuing, he may ruin the meat. One side may be overdone, and the other side raw. Likewise, we may not know the secret of sufficiency in Christ found in Philippians 4. We may talk a great deal about the book of Philippians, but not know the secret of experiencing Christ....In chapter four we have the secret and the power. On the one hand, Paul says, "I have learned the secret" (v. 12); on the other hand, he testifies, "I am able to do all things in Him who empowers me" (v. 13). (*Life-study of Philippians*, p. 243)

Today's Reading

How can we not worry but rejoice? In ourselves it is impossible. But if we have learned the secret of taking Christ as our person through His indwelling, it is so spontaneous. In the last part of [chapter 4], Paul tells us that he had learned the secret....Paul was not always so abounding, rich, and full. Many times he was abased. He was even hungry and had nothing to eat. Yet he had learned the secret both to be abased and to abound. Almost all of us have a kind of religious concept. If a brother becomes poor, we say that either he does not know how to manage himself, or he must be wrong with the Lord in some area. But how about the apostle Paul? Was God punishing him? He did suffer poverty, but not because he was wrong. Rather, that afforded him an opportunity to experience Christ. To him riches or poverty were of the same color. Whether the circumstances were good or not so good, he had learned the secret to rejoice in the Lord always.

Many times when I am worrying about something, the Lord rebukes me: "Why don't you enjoy Me as the One that takes care of you? Why not let Me worry for you?" When we learn the secret of taking Christ as our person, we learn to cast all our care upon Him. In Philippians, a book that speaks about Paul's circumstances, we see the secret for the Christian life and the practical way for the church life. That is, we must learn to take Christ as our person. We must let Him replace us. We cannot rejoice. We cannot be anxious for nothing. Our life is full of anxiety.

When we are in good circumstances, it is easy to praise the Lord. But when we are in bad circumstances, we can never praise the Lord. Today the sun is shining, but yesterday it was cloudy. This is the practical church life. Some days are full of sunshine, and some days are cloudy. But when we read Paul's life, we see that he had learned the secret. The secret is the indwelling Christ. Whether it is sunny or cloudy, whether the circumstances are good or bad, we have a wonderful Person living within us, bearing all our burdens. We must only learn to turn to Him and let Him be our person. (*The Indwelling Christ in the Canons of the New Testament,* pp. 138-140)

Further Reading: Life-study of Philippians, msg. 29; *The Indwelling Christ in the Canons of the New Testament,* ch. 15

Enlightenment and inspiration: _____

_____

_____

Morning Nourishment

Phil.   I know also how to be abased, and I know how to
4:12   abound; in everything and in all things I have
      learned the secret both to be filled and to hunger,
      both to abound and to lack.

1 Tim.   But if I delay, *I write* that you may know how one
3:15-16   ought to conduct himself in the house of God,
      which is the church of the living God, the pillar
      and base of the truth. And confessedly, great is the
      mystery of godliness: He who was manifested in
      the flesh, justified in the Spirit, seen by angels,
      preached among the nations, believed on in the
      world, taken up in glory.

Philippians 4 reveals to us that Christ is our secret and our power....In Greek the phrase *I have learned the secret* [in verse 12] means "I have been initiated." This may be illustrated by mathematics. When we teach a young student addition, subtraction, multiplication, and division, we initiate him by giving him the basic principles. In this way he learns the secret. Whenever he comes across a problem in mathematics, he knows the secret of how to solve it.

Christ is not only our power but our secret. We live by this power, and we live by this secret. Then whatever matter comes to us, we can solve it. Because we know the secret, we do not care whether we are rich or poor or whether we are abased or we abound....We have been initiated in Christ, with Christ, and by Christ. Because Christ is our secret, we know how to face any kind of situation. Whether people honor us or despise us, we know the secret and we have the power. Christ is our secret, and Christ is also our power. (*A General Sketch of the New Testament in the Light of Christ and the Church*, pp. 217-218)

Today's Reading

In verse 12...the words *I have learned the secret* are an interpretation of the Greek word which means "I have been initiated." The metaphor is that of a person being initiated into a secret society with instruction in its rudimentary principles. Paul had not only learned a secret; he had been initiated and had learned certain basic principles.

Among the Greeks there were a number of secret societies. Anyone who was to become a member of such a society had to learn the rudimentary principles of that society. Others had to initiate him into the society by instructing him in its principles. By using this metaphor, Paul was saying that a church, which is rather mysterious, has certain basic principles. After Paul was converted to Christ, he was in a sense initiated into the church life. This means that he was instructed in the secret of how to enjoy Christ, how to take Christ as life, how to live Christ, how to magnify Christ, how to gain Christ, and also how to have the church life. These are the rudimentary principles of the church life.

Although the church, the Body of Christ, is somewhat mysterious, the church definitely is not a secret society. On the contrary, the church is a bright city set on a hill. Furthermore, the church is open to all who are willing to come. But because the church has a mysterious aspect, there is the need of a spiritual initiation in order to learn the principles of the church life.

The basic principles of the church life are altogether different from the basic principles of the world. We may know all the rudimentary principles of the world and yet not know anything of the church life. Thus, when we are saved and come into the church, the Body of Christ, we need to be initiated by learning certain basic principles. The secret of the Body is to take Christ as our life, to live Christ, to pursue Christ, to gain Christ, to magnify Christ, and to express Christ. These are the basic principles of the church, the Body of Christ. As one who had been initiated into the Body, Paul had learned the secret. (*Life-study of Philippians*, pp. 244-245)

Further Reading: A General Sketch of the New Testament in the Light of Christ and the Church, ch. 18; Life-study of Philippians, msg. 29; A Thorough View of the Body of Christ, ch. 3

Enlightenment and inspiration: _____

_____

Morning Nourishment

Phil. Not that I speak according to lack, for I have
4:11-12 learned, in whatever circumstances I am, to be
content. I know also how to be abased, and I know
how to abound; in everything and in all things I
have learned the secret both to be filled and to
hunger, both to abound and to lack.

What a blessing it is to receive such a word concerning the
experience of Christ! I hope that the young people especially
will realize how blessed they are and will pray, "Lord, even in
my youth I desire to seek You, pursue You, and experience You
in the way presented in the book of Philippians. As far as the
normal experience and enjoyment of Christ are concerned, I
want to be today's Paul. I do not seek to be a great apostle,
evangelist, or a worker for Christ. But I do desire to be a normal
Christian experiencing You and enjoying You in everything day
by day, even in all things, for my whole life." May we all aspire
to enjoy Christ to such an extent. (*Life-study of Philippians,*
p. 253)

Today's Reading

In the Christian life we experience both night and day.
According to Genesis 1, night comes before day. When Paul was
abased, he was in the night, and when he was abounding, he
was in the day. Just as day follows night, night in turn will
follow day. This means that after the night of abasement came
the day of abounding. Paul realized, however, that this day
would eventually be followed by another night. We cannot
change the principle of God's universe. In the universe there
is night and day, day and night.

The Christian life does not stay on one level; it has many
ups and downs. It is normal to be up and down, down and up.
It is not normal to remain on one level and not experience ups
or downs. Likewise, it is not normal to experience day and not
night. Whose spiritual day is two hundred hours long? I do not
have such days. I have nights as well as days, downs as well

as ups. However, our account should be balanced: the ups should equal the downs, and the debit should equal the credit. When we have such a balance in our experience, we are normal.

According to the Lord's sovereign arrangement, we need both the ups and downs in order to experience Christ. I thank the Lord for all the valleys through which He has taken me. But with the valleys, there have also been hills. The Christian life is not one vast plain; it is a land with many hills and valleys. It is by the hills and valleys that we experience Christ.

Young people, do not dream that your life will be level and plain. On the contrary, you will face many valleys and many hills. You will encounter all kinds of circumstances. But in these circumstances you may apply Christ as your secret and experience Him. It is crucial that we learn to apply Christ.

Earlier we pointed out that in Philippians 4:12 Paul uses the puzzling expression "in everything and in all things." What is the difference between "everything" and "all things"? We experience one thing at a time. We cannot experience all things at once. Therefore, according to our experience in time, it is everything. But after a long period of experiences has gone by, the everything becomes all things.

We need to recall that the book of Philippians was written according to experience. In time we experience one thing after another. This fact is denoted by the word *everything*. But after a prolonged period of experience, the everything becomes all things. The words *in everything* refer to a particular time when we experience a certain thing of the Lord. The words *all things* refer to a broad range of experiences over a period of time. Paul could say that both on a particular occasion and on all occasions, both at a certain time and throughout the course of his life, he had learned the secret. Paul experienced Christ moment by moment. On the one hand, he experienced Christ in particular things at particular times. On the other hand, he experienced Christ in all things and at all times. (*Life-study of Philippians*, pp. 251-253)

Further Reading: Life-study of Philippians, msg. 29

Enlightenment and inspiration: _____

_____

Morning Nourishment

Phil. ...In everything and in all things I have learned
4:12-13 the secret both to be filled and to hunger, both
to abound and to lack. I am able to do all things
in Him who empowers me.

John Abide in Me and I in you....I am the vine; you
15:4-5 are the branches. He who abides in Me and I in
him, he bears much fruit; for apart from Me you
can do nothing.

Eph. To me, less than the least of all saints, was this
3:8 grace given to announce to the Gentiles the
unsearchable riches of Christ as the gospel.

Paul had been instructed in this secret so that he knew
both how to abound and how to be in want. He could do all
things in Him. It is sufficient simply to be in Him, for He
is all-inclusive and all-sufficient. For example, as we ride
in the car, we have complete trust in the car. Christ is more
sufficient and more inclusive than any car. Therefore, we
should put our full trust in Him. Whatever we do we should
do in Him, not in ourselves. We should do everything in
Him and by Him. This is the secret Paul learned and the
secret we need to learn today. We do not need more teaching, but more practice of this secret. We need to practice
doing everything in Him.

As we practice this secret, we should not have any
preference concerning what we do in Him. We, however,
may prefer to do certain things in Him, but not other
things....Because of all these preferences, we seldom turn
to Him and ask Him what He wants to do in a given
situation. But we need to pray, "Lord Jesus, do You want
me to do this? If so, show me Your way to do it, Lord." We
have Christ living in us, but we may not live by Him or do
things in Him. The secret in Philippians 4 is to do all things
in Him. The way to experience Christ is to do everything
in Him. (*The Experience of Christ,* p. 88)

Today's Reading

The issue of practicing the secret of doing everything in Christ is that for us, to live is Christ. Because we do all things in Christ, for us to live is Christ. The more we do things in Christ, the more we gain of Christ. This is a genuine, absolute enjoyment. However, not many Christians practice the secret of doing all things in Him. Rather, they like to attend meetings and hear messages. But the only way to live is to live by doing everything in Christ. This is the unique way to magnify Christ. In order to magnify Christ, we need to live by Christ and do everything in Christ. We can do all things in Him who empowers us. For example, as long as we are in the car, everything is all right, for the car with the driver can take us where we need to go. As we are riding along in the car, we can enjoy a pleasant time of sight-seeing. Learn to be quiet in Christ; He never makes a mistake. Sometimes, it may seem that He has made a mistake, but actually this is so that you may have a longer ride, enjoy more sight-seeing, and learn more lessons. The Christian life surely is a wonderful life.

As long as we do things in Christ, we shall experience Him, enjoy Him, and accumulate Him. This is the way to become rich in Christ and to have many rich experiences of Christ. If we all are rich in Christ, the meetings will be full of Christ. This is the Lord's recovery. For the recovery, we need to have a rich life in Christ to enrich all the meetings. This is the responsibility not only of the elders, but of all the saints, even the youngest and newest ones. We all need to practice living by Christ and doing all things in Christ. This is the secret that we all need to learn today. (*The Experience of Christ,* pp. 90-91)

Further Reading: The Experience of Christ, ch. 10; *Life-study of Philippians,* msg. 29

Enlightenment and inspiration: _____

_____

_____

Morning Nourishment

Phil.   ...I have learned, in whatever circumstances I am,
4:11-13 to be content....In everything and in all things I
have learned the secret....I am able to do all things
in Him who empowers me.

3:8-9 ...That I may gain Christ and be found in Him...

In Philippians 4:13 we find the secret to which Paul refers in verse 12. Here Paul says that he is in Christ, in the One who empowers him. In chapter three Paul testified that he pursued Christ in order to gain Him and be found in Him. Now in 4:13 Paul says that he is in Him. In Christ as the One who empowers him Paul could do all things. He could say, "Christ is my secret of sufficiency. As long as I have Him and as long as I am in Him, I can do all things in Him."

To appreciate Paul's word we need to join the phrase *in Him* in 4:13 to the same phrase in 3:9. In 3:9 Paul aspired to be found in Him; in 4:13 Paul declared that being in Him he could do all things in the One who empowered him. This is the secret.

Have you seen the secret? Do you have this secret? Our circumstances may change. In certain circumstances we may abound, and in others we may be abased. But whether we abound or are abased, the enjoyment of the Lord is the same. It may even have been the case that Paul enjoyed Christ more when he was abased than when he was abounding. Perhaps he enjoyed more of Christ when he was poor than when he was rich. This, however, is my understanding. Perhaps Paul would say, "No, I enjoy Christ equally when I am abased and when I am abounding. It makes no difference to me whether I am rich or poor, high or low. The enjoyment of Christ is the same."... Whether or not there was any difference in enjoyment,...it is certain that Paul had learned the secret. (*Life-study of Philippians,* pp. 249-250)

Today's Reading

When the church at Philippi did not have the opportunity to supply Paul, he was in want. He was humiliated and abased.

Do you think that during that time of abasement Paul was worrying? We may have the ground to answer this question with both a yes and a no. On the one hand, we can say that Paul was not worried, for he tells us that he had learned the secret both to be abased and to abound. On the other hand, there is an implication that, in referring to his situation, he must have had some human feeling of worry or anxiety. If Paul did not have any worry, why then did he refer to his situation? When he was in want, he must have had some feeling about it. Otherwise, he would not have told the Philippians that he rejoiced in the Lord greatly that "at length" they had caused their thinking for him to blossom anew. This positive word implies that, prior to receiving the supply through Epaphroditus, Paul was concerned.

If Paul did not have any feelings of worry or anxiety, why would he find it necessary to write such things in his Epistle to the Philippians? As a human being, Paul did undergo suffering with respect to material needs. Paul was not an angel, and he was not like a lifeless statue without feelings. No doubt, he had learned the secret of sufficiency in Christ. When he was in want and was tempted to worry about his situation, he applied this secret. Then, in his experience, this secret eliminated his worry. Therefore, he could have the boldness to testify that he knew both how to be abased and how to abound. The very fact that Paul knew how to be abased indicates that he experienced feelings of abasement. He knew what it was to have worry and anxiety in times of suffering. But at those times he applied the secret of the indwelling Christ. He applied the very Christ in whom he could be found. This Christ is real, living, near, available, and prevailing. This was the Christ who was Paul's secret. (*Life-study of Philippians,* pp. 250-251)

Further Reading: Life-study of Philippians, msg. 29; *The Experience of Christ,* ch. 10

Enlightenment and inspiration: _____

_____

_____

_____

Morning Nourishment

Phil. **Finally, brothers, what things are true, what**
4:8 **things are dignified, what things are righteous, what things are pure, what things are lovely, what things are well spoken of, if there is any virtue and if any praise, take account of these things.**

13 **I am able to do all things in Him who empowers me.**

Gal. **I am crucified with Christ; and** *it is* **no longer I** *who*
2:20 **live, but** *it is* **Christ** *who* **lives in me...**

4:19 **My children, with whom I travail again in birth until Christ is formed in you.**

Christ lives in the believers for them to be able to do all things in Him who empowers them. Paul says, "I can do all things in Him who empowers me" (Phil. 4:13). To be empowered by Christ is to be made dynamic inwardly. Christ dwells in us (Col. 1:27), and He empowers us, makes us dynamic, from within, not from without. By such inward empowering, Paul could do all things in Christ.

Paul was a person in Christ (2 Cor. 12:2) and he desired to be found in Christ by others (Phil. 3:9). In 4:13 he declared that he could do all things in Christ, the One who empowered him. This is an all-inclusive and concluding word of Paul's experience of Christ. It is the converse of the Lord's word concerning our organic relationship with Him in John 15:5, "Apart from Me you can do nothing." As long as we have Christ and are in Him, we can do all things in Him. (*The Conclusion of the New Testament,* p. 1554)

Today's Reading

In Christ as the One who empowers him Paul could do all things. Christ was his secret of sufficiency. By being in Him Paul could do all things in Him.

The "all things" in Philippians 4:13 refer to the things mentioned in verse 12 and to the virtues listed in verse 8. This means that the application of verse 13 is limited by the context of verses 8 through 13. By the empowering of Christ we can live a contented life (vv. 11-12) and be true, dignified, righteous, pure, lovely, and well spoken of. This means that we are persons in Christ, who empowers us to live out every kind of virtue. This is to live Christ, to magnify Christ in His virtues.

We need to realize that Paul's word about Christ as the empowering One specifically applies to Christ's empowering us to live Him as our human virtues and thereby to magnify Him in His unlimited greatness. The six virtues mentioned in 4:8 are actually the image of God. God created man in His image, that is, in His attributes of love, light, holiness, and righteousness. The fact that man was made in the image of God means that he was made in the form of love, light, holiness, and righteousness. The six items, whatever is true, dignified, righteous, pure, lovely, and well spoken of, are in these four divine attributes of love, light, holiness, and righteousness. This is the real virtue, for it is the expression of Christ. Christ empowers the believers to live Him and magnify Him in all these virtues.

To live a life of all these virtues is much more difficult than doing a Christian work. Many can preach the gospel, teach the Bible, and even establish churches, but they are not able to live this kind of life, a life full of the virtues of being true, dignified, righteous, pure, lovely, and well spoken of. In order to live Christ as our human virtues for the expression of the divine attributes, we need to be empowered by the indwelling Christ.

If we would experience Christ as the empowering One enabling us to do all things in Him, we need to let Him live in us (Gal. 2:20), be formed in us (Gal. 4:19), make His home in us (Eph. 3:17), and be magnified in us (Phil. 1:20). If we fail to do these things, He will not have the way to empower us. But when Christ lives in us, is formed in us, makes His home in us, and is magnified in us, the way is prepared for Him to empower us. Then, empowered by the indwelling Christ, we shall be able to do all the things spoken of in Philippians 4:8 through 12. (*The Conclusion of the New Testament*, pp. 1554-1555)

Further Reading: The Conclusion of the New Testament, msg. 143

Enlightenment and inspiration: _____

_____

_____

Hymns, #499

1   Oh, what a life! Oh, what a peace!
      The Christ who's all within me lives.
      With Him I have been crucified;
      This glorious fact to me He gives.
      Now it's no longer I that live,
      But Christ the Lord within me lives.

2   Oh, what a joy! Oh, what a rest!
      Christ now is being formed in me.
      His very nature and life divine
      In my whole being inwrought shall be.
      All that I am came to an end,
      And all of Christ is all to me.

3   Oh, what a thought! Oh, what a boast!
      Christ shall in me be magnified.
      In nothing shall I be ashamed,
      For He in all shall be applied.
      In woe or blessing, death or life,
      Through me shall Christ be testified.

4   Oh, what a prize! Oh, what a gain!
      Christ is the goal toward which I press.
      Nothing I treasure, nor aught desire,
      But Christ of all-inclusiveness.
      My hope, my glory, and my crown
      Is Christ, the One of peerlessness.

(Repeat the last two lines of each stanza)

Composition for prophecy with main point and sub-points: _____

_____

_____

_____

_____

_____

_____

_____

_____

_____

_____

_____

_____

_____

_____

_____

_____

_____

_____

_____

_____

_____

_____

_____

_____

_____

_____

_____

_____

_____

_____

_____

Taking Christ as Our Expectation

Scripture Reading: Phil. 3:20-21

Day 1   I. **The life which Paul lived in the experience of Christ was one that awaited the Savior, the Lord Jesus Christ, who would transfigure his body of humiliation, conforming it to the body of His glory; thus, he took the Christ whom he experienced as his expectation (3:20-21).**

II. **"For our commonwealth exists in the heavens, from which also we eagerly await a Savior, the Lord Jesus Christ" (v. 20):**

A. Our national life is not in any earthly country; our real citizenship, our true commonwealth, is in the heavens (Eph. 2:6, 19).

B. Because our citizenship is in the heavens, we should not be occupied with earthly things, the physical things needed for our existence (1 Tim. 6:6-10).

C. In dealing with our body, we should take care of our physical need but should not indulge in excessive physical enjoyment (Phil. 3:17-19; 1 Cor. 9:27).

D. As we await and love the Lord's glorious appearing, we should live a God-expressing and flesh-restricting life (Titus 2:12-13; Luke 21:34-36; 2 Tim. 4:8).

Day 2 III. **Christ "will transfigure the body of our humiliation to be conformed to the body of His glory, according to His operation by which He is able even to subject all things to Himself" (Phil. 3:21):**

A. We are waiting for Christ to come back so that we may be brought into the ultimate consummation of God's salvation—the transfiguration of our body:

1. In His salvation God first regenerated our spirit (John 3:6), now is transforming our

soul (Rom. 12:2), and consummately will transfigure our body for our glorification, making us the same as Christ in all three parts of our being (1 John 3:2).

2. The body of our humiliation is our natural body, made of worthless dust (Gen. 2:7) and damaged by sin, weakness, sickness, and death (Rom. 6:6; 7:24; 8:11).

3. The body of His glory is Christ's resurrected body, saturated with God's glory (Luke 24:26) and transcendent over corruption and death (Rom. 6:9).

4. The transfiguring of our body is accomplished by the Lord's great power, which subjects all things to Himself (Eph. 1:19-22); this is the almighty power in the universe.

Day 3   B. The transfiguration of our body is the redemption of our body for the full sonship of God (Rom. 8:23):

1. Although we have the divine Spirit as the firstfruits in our spirit, our body has not yet been saturated with the divine life; our body is still the flesh, linked to the old creation, and it is still a body of sin and death that is impotent in the things of God (6:6; 7:24; cf. 2 Cor. 5:4).

2. Hence, we groan together with the creation and eagerly await the glorious day when we will obtain the full sonship, the redemption and transfiguration of our body (Rom. 8:19-23).

3. The redemption of our body is through the saturation of the divine element by the sealing Spirit of God (Eph. 1:13; 4:30; 1 Cor. 1:30; Luke 21:28).

Day 4   C. The transfiguration of our body will be the glorification of our entire being (Rom. 8:30, 17; 1 Pet. 5:10a; 2 Tim. 2:10):

1. Objectively, glorification is that the redeemed believers will be brought into the

glory of God to participate in the glory of God (Heb. 2:10a; 1 Pet. 5:10a).

2. Subjectively, glorification is that the matured believers will manifest from within them, by their maturity in life, the glory of God as the element of their maturity in life (Rom. 8:17-18, 21; 2 Cor. 4:17):

a. The Lord is in us as the hope of glory to bring us into glory (Col. 1:27; Heb. 2:10a).

Day 5

b. At His coming back, on the one hand, He will come from the heavens with glory (Rev. 10:1; Matt. 25:31), and on the other hand, He will be glorified in His saints (2 Thes. 1:10):

1) His glory will be manifested from within His members, causing their body of humiliation to be transfigured into His glory, conforming it to the body of His glory (Phil. 3:21).

2) Thus, the unbelievers will marvel at Him, admire Him, wonder at Him, in us, the believers.

Day 6

3. We are on the way of being brought into glory by the sanctifying work of the Spirit; sanctification is the gradual process of glorification (Heb. 2:10-11; 1 Thes. 5:23; Eph. 5:26-27).

4. The reality of the believers' glorification is their gaining of God Himself—the glory of God is God Himself (Jer. 2:11; Eph. 1:17; 1 Cor. 2:8; 1 Pet. 4:14), and the manifestation of God is the glory of God (Acts 7:2):

a. The believers' entering into the glory of God to participate in the glory of God is their entering into God Himself to enjoy God Himself.

b. The believers' being transformed in the divine life today is God's being expressed in the believers as glory; hence, this daily transformation is from glory to glory (2 Cor. 3:18; 4:17).

c. The consummation of glory into which the believers will enter by transformation in life is that they will be glorified—their body will be redeemed, and they will thereby enter into the glory of God to fully enjoy God as glory (Rom. 8:21, 23, 30).

5. The believers' arriving at glorification is the climax of their maturity in the life of God and the climax of God's salvation in life (Heb. 6:1a; Rom. 5:10).

6. The believers' glorification is the accomplishment of God's economy for the satisfaction of God's desire:

a. The full expression of the believers' glorification is the New Jerusalem, which will be manifested in glory (Rev. 21:10-11).

b. This is the full expression in eternity of God's becoming a man in humanity and of man's being conformed to God in divinity.

c. This is what God desires and is His heart's delight, and this is also what God is waiting for in His good pleasure (Eph. 1:5).

Morning Nourishment

Titus ...We should live soberly and righteously and
2:12-13 godly in the present age, awaiting the blessed
        hope, even the appearing of the glory of our great
        God and Savior, Jesus Christ.

Phil. For our commonwealth exists in the heavens,
3:20 from which also we eagerly await a Savior, the
      Lord Jesus Christ.

Eph. So then you are no longer strangers and sojourn-
2:19 ers, but you are fellow citizens with the saints and
     members of the household of God.

The life which Paul lived in the experience of Christ was one
that awaited the Savior, the Lord Jesus Christ, who would come
from the heavens to transfigure his body of humiliation, conforming it to the body of His glory. Thus, he took the Christ whom
he experienced as his expectation. (*Life Lessons,* vol. 3, p. 39)

Today's Reading

In Philippians 3:20 Paul goes on to say, "For our commonwealth exists in the heavens, from which also we eagerly await
a Savior, the Lord Jesus Christ." The Greek word rendered
commonwealth may also be rendered "citizenship" or "associa-
tions of life." Our national life is not in any earthly country; it
is in the heavens. Our real citizenship, our true commonwealth, is in the heavens. Sometimes as I am traveling, people
ask me where I come from. Although I may have to tell them
that I come from China, I prefer to say that I come from the
heavens and that my citizenship is in the heavens.

Because our citizenship is in the heavens, we should not be
occupied with earthly things, with the physical things needed
for our existence. We should not place such a high value on
material things. This does not mean, of course, that we should
not have proper food, clothing, housing, and transportation. We
definitely need these things. But anything that goes beyond
need falls into the category of indulgence. Such indulgence is

to be condemned. If we love the earthly things needed for human life, this is an indication that we do not treasure our heavenly citizenship. May we all remember that our citizenship is in the heavens and that we are a heavenly people sojourning on earth. If we have food, clothing, housing, and transportation to maintain life, we should be content. Let us not indulge ourselves in any earthly, material things.

I believe that now we can grasp Paul's basic thought in Philippians 3. In this chapter Paul instructs us both concerning how to deal with the soul and how to deal with the body. To deal with the soul, we must count as loss all religious, philosophical, and cultural things so that Christ may occupy our entire being and that we may gain Him to the uttermost. To deal with our body, we should take care of our physical need, but not indulge in excessive physical enjoyment. Our aim should be to care for the body in a proper way that it may be healthy for the Lord's expression. But our intention should not be to glorify the physical body through the over-enjoyment of physical things. Our body is not to be glorified in this way, but is to be glorified at the time of the Lord's coming back. At that time, He will transfigure our body of humiliation. Thus, we are waiting for Christ to come back that we may be brought into the ultimate consummation of God's salvation—the transfiguration of our body.

While we are waiting for the Lord's coming, we should take care of our physical needs without indulging in material things. At the same time, we should deal with our soul, counting as loss all religious, philosophical, and cultural things so that our soul may be transformed in full. Day by day, we are undergoing the process of transformation in our soul as we are waiting for the Lord to come to transfigure our body and thereby to bring us into the ultimate consummation of God's salvation. (*Life-study of Philippians*, pp. 213-215)

Further Reading: Life Lessons, lsn. 29; *Life-study of Philippians*, msg. 25; *Life-study of Titus*, msg. 4

Enlightenment and inspiration: _____

_____

_____

Morning Nourishment

Phil. 3:21 Who will transfigure the body of our humiliation to be conformed to the body of His glory, according to His operation by which He is able even to subject all things to Himself.

John 3:6 ...That which is born of the Spirit is spirit.

Rom. 12:2 ...Be transformed by the renewing of the mind...

1 John 3:2 Beloved, now we are children of God, and it has not yet been manifested what we will be. We know that if He is manifested, we will be like Him because we will see Him even as He is.

The redemption of our body is the transfiguration of our body of humiliation (Phil. 3:21). Our body has been humiliated by the fall. By the fall, sin invaded our body. Therefore, today in the members of our body, according to Romans 7, there is an evil thing called sin. Sin dwells in us (v. 20) and has become a law of sin dwelling in the members of our body (v. 23). This sin brings in death, and death implies weakness and sickness. Our body has been humiliated by sin, by weakness, by sickness, and eventually by death. Our body is not something glorious. It is something humiliated with mainly these four things—sin, weakness, sickness, and death.

Actually, we human beings are not living. Everybody is dying. Eventually, all of us will die. We are dying persons. This is a kind of humiliation. But the redemption of our body will change the nature and the condition of our body. That change will be a transfiguration. Philippians 3:21 says that Christ "will transfigure the body of our humiliation to be conformed to the body of His glory, according to His operation by which He is able even to subject all things to Himself." (*The Apostles' Teaching*, p. 87)

Today's Reading

From the heavens we are eagerly awaiting a Savior, the

Lord Jesus Christ, who "will transfigure the body of our humiliation to be conformed to the body of His glory, according to His operation by which He is able even to subject all things to Himself." The transfiguration of our body will be the ultimate consummation of God's salvation. In His salvation God first regenerated our spirit (John 3:6), now He is transforming our soul (Rom. 12:2), and, consummately, He will transfigure our body, making us the same as Christ in all three parts of our being.

In verse 21 Paul refers to our body as "the body of our humiliation." This describes our natural body, made of worthless dust (Gen. 2:7) and damaged by sin, weakness, sickness, and death (Rom. 6:6; 7:24; 8:11). But one day this body will be transfigured and conformed to the body of Christ's glory. Christ's body of glory is His resurrected body, saturated with God's glory (Luke 24:26) and transcendent over corruption and death (Rom. 6:9).

No matter how we may feed and clothe our body and no matter what kind of automobile we use to transport it or dwelling place to house it, it is still a body of humiliation. You may allow your body to rest on the best and most expensive bed, but it is nonetheless a body of humiliation. However, we should not hate or despise our body. If we despise our body, we shall practice asceticism. In a very real sense, we should love our body for the Lord's sake. We need to care for the body without allowing it to indulge itself. One day, the Lord Jesus will come and transfigure the body of humiliation and conform it to the body of His glory.

In verse 21 Paul says that the transfiguration of the body of humiliation is "according to His operation by which He is able even to subject all things to Himself." The transfiguration of our body is by the great power which subjects all things to the Lord (Eph. 1:19-22). This is the almighty power in the whole universe. (*Life-study of Philippians,* pp. 214-215)

Further Reading: The Apostles' Teaching, ch. 8; *Life-study of Philippians,* msg. 25

Enlightenment and inspiration: _____
_____

Morning Nourishment

Rom. And not only *so*, but we ourselves also, who have
8:23 the firstfruits of the Spirit, even we ourselves
groan in ourselves, eagerly awaiting sonship, the
redemption of our body.

Eph. In whom you also, having heard the word of the
1:13 truth, the gospel of your salvation, in Him also
believing, you were sealed with the Holy Spirit
of the promise.

4:30 And do not grieve the Holy Spirit of God, in whom
you were sealed unto the day of redemption.

Glorification is the saturating of God's glory from within
the believers like the inking of the sealing which the believers
received at their salvation (Eph. 1:13; 4:30). When a seal with
much ink is applied to some pages of paper, it will saturate
through to the last page. Ephesians 4:30 says that we are
sealed with the Spirit unto the day of redemption. *Unto*
means "resulting in." This inking of the sealing Spirit will
eventually result in the redemption of our body at our glorification.

Such a glorification, the redemption of our body, is the full
enjoyment of our sonship (Rom. 8:23). We are the sons of God,
but our body has not yet been "sonized." Our body will be
sonized when it is redeemed. To be transfigured, to be redeemed, is to be sonized. We were born sons of God at the
time of our regeneration, but at that time only our spirit was
sonized. Regeneration is the first step of sonizing. Organic
feeding, sanctification, renewing, transformation, building,
and conformation are the following steps. The last step is
the sonizing of our body. (*The Divine and Mystical Realm*,
pp. 69-70)

Today's Reading

The redemption of our body is through the saturation of
the divine element by the sealing of the Spirit of God (Rom.
8:23; Eph. 4:30; 1 Cor. 1:30; Luke 21:28). We believers are

being saturated with the divine element. Outwardly, we may look the same as the unbelievers. But inwardly, something hidden is going on within us. Inwardly, we are being saturated with the divine element of God's life. This saturating is by the sealing of the Spirit of God. When a piece of paper is sealed with a seal, the ink on the image of the seal saturates the paper. Within us the sealing of the Spirit of God is going on.

Ephesians 1:13-14 and 4:30 speak of this sealing. The Holy Spirit is the sealing ink, and God has sealed us with the Spirit as the sealing ink. This sealing is going on unto the redemption of our body....Someone who has been recently saved has a small amount of the divine ink within him. As he grows in the divine life, the divine ink permeates and saturates him. Eventually, this saturation will reach his body. That will be the time of his rapture, which is the redemption of his body. We need to be permeated and saturated with the Spirit until the redemption of our body.

The redemption of our body to transfigure the nature and the condition of our body of humiliation is also the full sonship of God. We are sons of God today because we have the very reality of the sonship of God in our spirit. But today we do not have the sonship of God in our body. Our body has not yet entered into divinity. But one day our body will enter into divinity. Divinity is now saturating our being. One day this saturation will reach a consummation, and our entire body will be consummated in divinity. By that time we will enjoy the full sonship. None of the unbelievers can discern that we are the sons of God today. To them we are the same as they are. But according to Romans 8, one day the sons of God will be manifested. Everyone will be able to see that we are the sons of God. The redemption of our body is the full sonship of God. (*The Apostles' Teaching,* pp. 86-88)

Further Reading: The Divine and Mystical Realm, ch. 5; *The Apostles' Teaching,* ch. 8; *The Secret of God's Organic Salvation: "The Spirit Himself with Our Spirit,"* ch. 5

Enlightenment and inspiration: _____

_____

_____

Morning Nourishment

2 Cor. For our momentary lightness of affliction works
4:17   out for us, more and more surpassingly, an eternal
       weight of glory.

1 Pet. But the God of all grace, He who has called you
5:10   into His eternal glory in Christ Jesus, after you
       have suffered a little while, will Himself perfect,
       establish, strengthen, *and* ground *you*.

Rom.   And if children, heirs also; on the one hand, heirs
8:17-18 of God; on the other, joint heirs with Christ, if
       indeed we suffer with *Him* that we may also be
       glorified with *Him*. For I consider that the suffer-
       ings of this present time are not worthy to be
       compared with the coming glory to be revealed
       upon us.

Second Corinthians 4:17 tells us that the momentary lightness of affliction which we suffer now for the Lord is working out for us, more and more surpassingly, an eternal weight of glory. Today if we endure sufferings for the Lord, this will increase the weight of glory that we will receive from the Lord. Romans 8:17 also says that if we suffer with the Lord, we will also be glorified with Him. These all prove that the degree of glory we are to receive in the future is built up by us today.

We thank the Lord that we have been regenerated. We have Him in us as our life and our supply. We daily receive from Him the supply for us to be metabolically transformed. Our being transformed in this way every day is our growth in life. And our growth in life is the building up of the degree of our glorification. If we have not been living out the glory of the Lord on the earth, how can we expect that He will suddenly put His glory upon us at His coming back? Therefore, today if we are living out God on the earth, God becomes the glory upon us. When the Lord comes back, He will say, "Well done, good and faithful slave....Enter into the joy of your master" (Matt. 25:23). This is to enter into glory. (*God's Salvation in Life*, p. 66)

Today's Reading

Objectively, glorification is that the redeemed believers will be brought into the glory of God to participate in the glory of God (Heb. 2:10a; 1 Pet. 5:10a). This is the objective definition of glorification. It seems that today the glory of God is far away in the heavens, and we, the redeemed ones, are here on the earth; there is a great distance separating the two. Sometimes we feel that we are very far away from the glory of God, but this kind of feeling is only partially accurate.

Subjectively, glorification is that the matured believers will manifest from within them, by their maturity in life, the glory of God as the element of their maturity in life (Rom. 8:17-18, 21; 2 Cor. 4:17). This is the subjective definition of glorification. We may use an example to illustrate subjective glorification. When a flower in the garden begins to grow, it is just a little green tender sprout. The more it grows, however, the more mature it becomes. Gradually flower buds begin to appear. If you continue to water the plant, it will grow more. After a while the plant will blossom. When the flowers are in full bloom, that is the glorification. The glory of the flowers does not come from without; rather, it grows out from within. Therefore, on the one hand, we have a hope of glory in that Christ is coming to glorify us. This is objective. On the other hand, we are being transformed into the image of the Lord, with glory upon glory, that is, from glory to glory (2 Cor. 3:18). This is not glory descending on us; rather, it is glory growing out from within us. In springtime when all kinds of flowers are blooming, none of these beautiful flowers descend on the stems from the outside. Rather, they grow out from within the plant itself. If you are a lover of the Lord, and if you let the Lord live in you and you live by the Lord, then when people observe you, they will see the glory of God upon you. This glory is subjective and not objective. (*God's Salvation in Life,* pp. 63-64)

Further Reading: God's Salvation in Life, ch. 4

Enlightenment and inspiration: _____

_____

Morning Nourishment

Heb. **For it was fitting for Him, for whom are all things**
2:10-11 **and through whom are all things, in leading many**
sons into glory, to make the Author of their salva-
tion perfect through sufferings. For both He who
sanctifies and those who are being sanctified are
all of One, for which cause He is not ashamed to
call them brothers.

1 Thes. **And the God of peace Himself sanctify you wholly,**
5:23 **and may your spirit and soul and body be pre-**
served complete, without blame, at the coming of
our Lord Jesus Christ.

In 1 Thessalonians 5:23, Paul expressed the desire for our
whole being to be sanctified, that is, to be brought into glory in
full. How much we are in the glory depends upon how much
we have been sanctified. We are on the way of being brought
into glory by the sanctifying work of the Spirit. The more we
are sanctified, the more we enter into glory. Our being fully
sanctified, not only in our spirit but also in our soul and even
in our body, means our whole being has been reconstituted with
the divine element. Our spirit, soul, and body will be reconstituted, sanctified wholly, and that will be our glorification.

Sanctification is the gradual process of glorification. The
more we are sanctified, the more we are made holy and the
more we feel that we are in the glory. When the Spirit corrects
us, He supplies us and transfuses us with all the riches of
Christ to sanctify us. Then we have the feeling that we are
glorified. Thus, sanctification consummates in the believers'
glorification. (*The Spirit with Our Spirit,* pp. 115-116)

Today's Reading

Hebrews 2:10 says that the Lord as the Author, or Captain,
of God's salvation will lead many sons into glory. Then verse 11
speaks of the One who sanctifies and those who are being
sanctified. When I considered these two verses, my eyes were
opened to see that sanctification is for sonship. This is new light.

When I saw this, I entered into a fuller understanding of Ephesians 1:4-5. Verse 4 says "to be holy," and verse 5 says "unto sonship." We need to put these two phrases together—"to be holy unto sonship." This shows us again that sanctification is for sonship....To be holy results in the sonship. God's sonship comes to us through the Holy Spirit's sanctification....Divine sanctification is not for sinless perfection nor is it merely for a change of our position. It is for the sonship and results in the sonship. We call it the divine sanctification because it is a matter of the Spirit Himself. It is a matter of the Triune God.

Our full transformation will one day consummate in our glorification. That will be the work of the sanctifying Spirit to glorify us in our body. Another thing that bothers us besides our soul is our poor, vile body. Lust, weakness, sickness, and death are present in our corrupted body. Our body is really vile, but one day we will be glorified and transfigured in our body (Phil. 3:21). Our spirit has been regenerated, our soul is being transformed, and our body will be transfigured, changed into a glorious body with no more lust, weakness, sickness, or death. This is the glorifying sanctification.

Now we have seen the proper teaching of the New Testament concerning sanctification. Sanctification is the hinge of God's carrying out of His eternal economy. The sanctifying Spirit in God's sanctification first sought us out and then regenerated us, making us sons of God....God created everything according to its kind. Man, however, was created according to God's kind because he was created in God's image (Gen. 1:26). Later, we men were born of God, not only bearing God's image but also having God's life and nature. Thus, we become God in life and in nature, but not in the Godhead. This is what the sonship means. (*The Issue of the Dispensing of the Processed Trinity and the Transmitting of the Transcending Christ,* pp. 22, 25-26)

Further Reading: The Spirit with Our Spirit, ch. 11; The Issue of the Dispensing of the Processed Trinity and the Transmitting of the Transcending Christ, ch. 2

Enlightenment and inspiration: _____

_____

Morning Nourishment

Col.
1:27 To whom God willed to make known what are the riches of the glory of this mystery among the Gentiles, which is Christ in you, the hope of glory.

2 Thes.
1:10 When He comes to be glorified in His saints and to be marveled at in all those who have believed...

2 Cor.
3:18 But we all with unveiled face, beholding and reflecting like a mirror the glory of the Lord, are being transformed into the same image from glory to glory, even as from the Lord Spirit.

Rev.
21:10-11 And he...showed me the holy city, Jerusalem, coming down out of heaven from God, having the glory of God....

The redemption of our body, which is the transfiguration of our body of humiliation, will be the glorification of our entire being (Rom. 8:30, 17; 2 Thes. 1:10; 1 Pet. 5:10; 2 Tim. 2:10; Heb. 2:10). This means that our entire being will be saturated with the glory of the divine life.

Second Thessalonians 1:10 says that Christ will come to glorify Himself in us....On the one hand, Christ's coming is from the heavens. On the other hand, Christ's coming is from within us. Today Christ is first in the heavens and then in us. When He comes, He will come from these two directions. He will come from the heavens above to the earth. He also will come from within us. He is coming out from our spirit to appear in our body. The appearance of Christ from within us is His coming. This kind of coming is His glorification. Christ in us is a mystery. He is in us as the hope of glory (Col. 1:27). One day this hope will be manifested, and that will be our glory. When the inner hope is manifested, He will become the outer glorification. In that day Christ will glorify Himself in us. That is our glorification, and in our glorification Christ will be glorified. (*The Apostles' Teaching,* p. 88)

Today's Reading

The reality of the believers' glorification is their gaining of

God Himself. Without God, we do not have glory. When we gain God, we are glorified. The measure of God that we have determines the measure of our glory.

The believers' entering into the glory of God to participate in the glory of God is their entering into God Himself to enjoy God Himself. God does not give us great glory objectively merely for us to make a display. God manifests Himself in us that we may enjoy Him. The more we enjoy God and the more God we have in us, the more we have His glory. The more we enjoy God, the more we are full of glory....To you, you are simply enjoying God. To others, however, you are manifesting the glory of God. You are glorifying God, and God is expressed through you.

The believers' being transformed in the divine life today is God's being expressed in the believers as glory; hence, this daily transformation is from glory to glory (2 Cor. 3:18b). The practical, subjective glory of God in us is a glory that progresses from one degree to another degree. This expressing of God is progressive and advancing; hence, it is from glory to glory.

The consummation of glory into which the believers will enter by transformation in life is that they will be glorified— their body will be redeemed, and they will thereby enter into the glory of God to fully enjoy God as glory (Rom. 8:21, 23, 30). The ultimate result of the believers' transformation in life is that they gain God and enjoy God. This is the principle today, and it will be the same principle in the future.

Glorification is the ultimate consummation of God's salvation in life. It is God's salvation in life saving us to the uttermost through regeneration, transformation, conformation, and glorification. The believers' arriving at glorification is the climax of their maturity in the life of God....The believers' reaching the peak of glorification is their reaching the climax of God's salvation in life. (*God's Salvation in Life,* pp. 67-69)

Further Reading: The Apostles' Teaching, ch. 8; *God's Salvation in Life,* ch. 4

Enlightenment and inspiration: _____

_____

_____

_____

Hymns, #948

1   Myst'ry hid from ages now revealed to me,
     'Tis the Christ of God's reality.
     He embodies God, and He is life to me,
     And the glory of my hope He'll be.

     Glory, glory, Christ is life in me!
          Glory, glory, what a hope is He!
     Now within my spirit He's the mystery!
          Then the glory He will be to me.

2   In my spirit He regenerated me,
          In my soul He's now transforming me.
     He will change my body like unto His own,
          Wholly making me the same as He.

3   Now in life and nature He is one with me;
          Then in Him, the glory, I will be;
     I'll enjoy His presence for eternity
          With Him in complete conformity.

*Composition for prophecy with main point and
sub-points:* _____

_____

_____

_____

_____

_____

_____

_____

_____

_____

_____

_____

_____

_____

_____

_____

_____

_____

_____

_____

_____

_____

_____

_____

_____

_____

_____

_____

_____

_____

_____

_____

Reading Schedule for the Recovery Version of the New Testament with Footnotes

Wk.	Lord's Day	Monday	Tuesday	Wednesday	Thursday	Friday	Saturday
1	Matt 1:1-2	1:3-7	1:8-17	1:18-25	2:1-23	3:1-6	3:7-17
2	4:1-11	4:12-25	5:1-4	5:5-12	5:13-20	5:21-26	5:27-48
3	6:1-8	6:9-18	6:19-34	7:1-12	7:13-29	8:1-13	8:14-22
4	8:23-34	9:1-13	9:14-17	9:18-34	9:35—10:5	10:6-25	10:26-42
5	11:1-15	11:16-30	12:1-14	12:15-32	12:33-42	12:43—13:2	13:3-12
6	13:13-30	13:31-43	13:44-58	14:1-13	14:14-21	14:22-36	15:1-20
7	15:21-31	15:32-39	16:1-12	16:13-20	16:21-28	17:1-13	17:14-27
8	18:1-14	18:15-22	18:23-35	19:1-15	19:16-30	20:1-16	20:17-34
9	21:1-11	21:12-22	21:23-32	21:33-46	22:1-22	22:23-33	22:34-46
10	23:1-12	23:13-39	24:1-14	24:15-31	24:32-51	25:1-13	25:14-30
11	25:31-46	26:1-16	26:17-35	26:36-46	26:47-64	26:65-75	27:1-26
12	27:27-44	27:45-56	27:57—28:15	28:16-20	Mark 1:1	1:2-6	1:7-13
13	1:14-28	1:29-45	2:1-12	2:13-28	3:1-19	3:20-35	4:1-25
14	4:26-41	5:1-20	5:21-43	6:1-29	6:30-56	7:1-23	7:24-37
15	8:1-26	8:27—9:1	9:2-29	9:30-50	10:1-16	10:17-34	10:35-52
16	11:1-16	11:17-33	12:1-27	12:28-44	13:1-13	13:14-37	14:1-26
17	14:27-52	14:53-72	15:1-15	15:16-47	16:1-8	16:9-20	Luke 1:1-4
18	1:5-25	1:26-46	1:47-56	1:57-80	2:1-8	2:9-20	2:21-39
19	2:40-52	3:1-20	3:21-38	4:1-13	4:14-30	4:31-44	5:1-26
20	5:27—6:16	6:17-38	6:39-49	7:1-17	7:18-23	7:24-35	7:36-50
21	8:1-15	8:16-25	8:26-39	8:40-56	9:1-17	9:18-26	9:27-36
22	9:37-50	9:51-62	10:1-11	10:12-24	10:25-37	10:38-42	11:1-13
23	11:14-26	11:27-36	11:37-54	12:1-12	12:13-21	12:22-34	12:35-48
24	12:49-59	13:1-9	13:10-17	13:18-30	13:31—14:6	14:7-14	14:15-24
25	14:25-35	15:1-10	15:11-21	15:22-32	16:1-13	16:14-22	16:23-31
26	17:1-19	17:20-37	18:1-14	18:15-30	18:31-43	19:1-10	19:11-27

Reading Schedule for the Recovery Version of the New Testament with Footnotes

Wk.	Lord's Day	Monday	Tuesday	Wednesday	Thursday	Friday	Saturday
27	☐ Luke 19:28-48	☐ 20:1-19	☐ 20:20-38	☐ 20:39—21:4	☐ 21:5-27	☐ 21:28-38	☐ 22:1-20
28	☐ 22:21-38	☐ 22:39-54	☐ 22:55-71	☐ 23:1-43	☐ 23:44-56	☐ 24:1-12	☐ 24:13-35
29	☐ 24:36-53	☐ John 1:1-13	☐ 1:14-18	☐ 1:19-34	☐ 1:35-51	☐ 2:1-11	☐ 2:12-22
30	☐ 2:23—3:13	☐ 3:14-21	☐ 3:22-36	☐ 4:1-14	☐ 4:15-26	☐ 4:27-42	☐ 4:43-54
31	☐ 5:1-16	☐ 5:17-30	☐ 5:31-47	☐ 6:1-15	☐ 6:16-31	☐ 6:32-51	☐ 6:52-71
32	☐ 7:1-9	☐ 7:10-24	☐ 7:25-36	☐ 7:37-52	☐ 7:53—8:11	☐ 8:12-27	☐ 8:28-44
33	☐ 8:45-59	☐ 9:1-13	☐ 9:14-34	☐ 9:35—10:9	☐ 10:10-30	☐ 10:31—11:4	☐ 11:5-22
34	☐ 11:23-40	☐ 11:41-57	☐ 12:1-11	☐ 12:12-24	☐ 12:25-36	☐ 12:37-50	☐ 13:1-11
35	☐ 13:12-30	☐ 13:31-38	☐ 14:1-6	☐ 14:7-20	☐ 14:21-31	☐ 15:1-11	☐ 15:12-27
36	☐ 16:1-15	☐ 16:16-33	☐ 17:1-5	☐ 17:6-13	☐ 17:14-24	☐ 17:25—18:11	☐ 18:12-27
37	☐ 18:28-40	☐ 19:1-16	☐ 19:17-30	☐ 19:31-42	☐ 20:1-13	☐ 20:14-18	☐ 20:19-22
38	☐ 20:23-31	☐ 21:1-14	☐ 21:15-22	☐ 21:23-25	☐ Acts 1:1-8	☐ 1:9-14	☐ 1:15-26
39	☐ 2:1-13	☐ 2:14-21	☐ 2:22-36	☐ 2:37-41	☐ 2:42-47	☐ 3:1-18	☐ 3:19—4:22
40	☐ 4:23-37	☐ 5:1-16	☐ 5:17-32	☐ 5:33-42	☐ 6:1—7:1	☐ 7:2-29	☐ 7:30-60
41	☐ 8:1-13	☐ 8:14-25	☐ 8:26-40	☐ 9:1-19	☐ 9:20-43	☐ 10:1-16	☐ 10:17-33
42	☐ 10:34-48	☐ 11:1-18	☐ 11:19-30	☐ 12:1-25	☐ 13:1-12	☐ 13:13-43	☐ 13:44—14:5
43	☐ 14:6-28	☐ 15:1-12	☐ 15:13-34	☐ 15:35—16:5	☐ 16:6-18	☐ 16:19-40	☐ 17:1-18
44	☐ 17:19-34	☐ 18:1-17	☐ 18:18-28	☐ 19:1-20	☐ 19:21-41	☐ 20:1-12	☐ 20:13-38
45	☐ 21:1-14	☐ 21:15-26	☐ 21:27-40	☐ 22:1-21	☐ 22:22-29	☐ 22:30—23:11	☐ 23:12-15
46	☐ 23:16-30	☐ 23:31—24:21	☐ 24:22—25:5	☐ 25:6-27	☐ 26:1-13	☐ 26:14-32	☐ 27:1-26
47	☐ 27:27—28:10	☐ 28:11-22	☐ 28:23-31	☐ Rom 1:1-2	☐ 1:3-7	☐ 1:8-17	☐ 1:18-25
48	☐ 1:26—2:10	☐ 2:11-29	☐ 3:1-20	☐ 3:21-31	☐ 4:1-12	☐ 4:13-25	☐ 5:1-11
49	☐ 5:12-17	☐ 5:18—6:5	☐ 6:6-11	☐ 6:12-23	☐ 7:1-12	☐ 7:13-25	☐ 8:1-2
50	☐ 8:3-6	☐ 8:7-13	☐ 8:14-25	☐ 8:26-39	☐ 9:1-18	☐ 9:19—10:3	☐ 10:4-15
51	☐ 10:16—11:10	☐ 11:11-22	☐ 11:23-36	☐ 12:1-3	☐ 12:4-21	☐ 13:1-14	☐ 14:1-12
52	☐ 14:13-23	☐ 15:1-13	☐ 15:14-33	☐ 16:1-5	☐ 16:6-24	☐ 16:25-27	☐ I Cor 1:1-4

Reading Schedule for the Recovery Version of the New Testament with Footnotes

Wk.	Lord's Day	Monday	Tuesday	Wednesday	Thursday	Friday	Saturday
53	I Cor 1:5-9	1:10-17	1:18-31	2:1-5	2:6-10	2:11-16	3:1-9
54	3:10-13	3:14-23	4:1-9	4:10-21	5:1-13	6:1-11	6:12-20
55	7:1-16	7:17-24	7:25-40	8:1-13	9:1-15	9:16-27	10:1-4
56	10:5-13	10:14-33	11:1-6	11:7-16	11:17-26	11:27-34	12:1-11
57	12:12-22	12:23-31	13:1-13	14:1-12	14:13-25	14:26-33	14:34-40
58	15:1-19	15:20-28	15:29-34	15:35-49	15:50-58	16:1-9	16:10-24
59	II Cor 1:1-4	1:5-14	1:15-22	1:23—2:11	2:12-17	3:1-6	3:7-11
60	3:12-18	4:1-6	4:7-12	4:13-18	5:1-8	5:9-15	5:16-21
61	6:1-13	6:14—7:4	7:5-16	8:1-15	8:16-24	9:1-15	10:1-6
62	10:7-18	11:1-15	11:16-33	12:1-10	12:11-21	13:1-10	13:11-14
63	Gal 1:1-5	1:6-14	1:15-24	2:1-13	2:14-21	3:1-4	3:5-14
64	3:15-22	3:23-29	4:1-7	4:8-20	4:21-31	5:1-12	5:13-21
65	5:22-26	6:1-10	6:11-15	6:16-18	Eph 1:1-3	1:4-6	1:7-10
66	1:11-14	1:15-18	1:19-23	2:1-5	2:6-10	2:11-14	2:15-18
67	2:19-22	3:1-7	3:8-13	3:14-18	3:19-21	4:1-4	4:5-10
68	4:11-16	4:17-24	4:25-32	5:1-10	5:11-21	5:22-26	5:27-33
69	6:1-9	6:10-14	6:15-18	6:19-24	Phil 1:1-7	1:8-18	1:19-26
70	1:27—2:4	2:5-11	2:12-16	2:17-30	3:1-6	3:7-11	3:12-16
71	3:17-21	4:1-9	4:10-23	Col 1:1-8	1:9-13	1:14-23	1:24-29
72	2:1-7	2:8-15	2:16-23	3:1-4	3:5-15	3:16-25	4:1-18
73	I Thes 1:1-3	1:4-10	2:1-12	2:13—3:5	3:6-13	4:1-10	4:11—5:11
74	5:12-28	II Thes 1:1-12	2:1-17	3:1-18	I Tim 1:1-2	1:3-4	1:5-14
75	1:15-20	2:1-7	2:8-15	3:1-13	3:14—4:5	4:6-16	5:1-25
76	6:1-10	6:11-21	II Tim 1:1-10	1:11-18	2:1-15	2:16-26	3:1-13
77	3:14—4:8	4:9-22	Titus 1:1-4	1:5-16	2:1-15	3:1-8	3:9-15
78	Philem 1:1-11	1:12-25	Heb 1:1-2	1:3-5	1:6-14	2:1-9	2:10-18

Reading Schedule for the Recovery Version of the New Testament with Footnotes

Wk.	Lord's Day	Monday	Tuesday	Wednesday	Thursday	Friday	Saturday
79	Heb 3:1-6	3:7-19	4:1-9	4:10-13	4:14-16	5:1-10	5:11—6:3
80	6:4-8	6:9-20	7:1-10	7:11-28	8:1-6	8:7-13	9:1-4
81	9:5-14	9:15-28	10:1-18	10:19-28	10:29-39	11:1-6	11:7-19
82	11:20-31	11:32-40	12:1-2	12:3-13	12:14-17	12:18-26	12:27-29
83	13:1-7	13:8-12	13:13-15	13:16-25	James1:1-8	1:9-18	1:19-27
84	2:1-13	2:14-26	3:1-18	4:1-10	4:11-17	5:1-12	5:13-20
85	I Pet 1:1-2	1:3-4	1:5	1:6-9	1:10-12	1:13-17	1:18-25
86	2:1-3	2:4-8	2:9-17	2:18-25	3:1-13	3:14-22	4:1-6
87	4:7-16	4:17-19	5:1-4	5:5-9	5:10-14	II Pet 1:1-2	1:3-4
88	1:5-8	1:9-11	1:12-18	1:19-21	2:1-3	2:4-11	2:12-22
89	3:1-6	3:7-9	3:10-12	3:13-15	3:16	3:17-18	I John 1:1-2
90	1:3-4	1:5	1:6	1:7	1:8-10	2:1-2	2:3-11
91	2:12-14	2:15-19	2:20-23	2:24-27	2:28-29	3:1-5	3:6-10
92	3:11-18	3:19-24	4:1-6	4:7-11	4:12-15	4:16—5:3	5:4-13
93	5:14-17	5:18-21	II John 1:1-3	1:4-9	1:10-13	III John 1:1-6	1:7-14
94	Jude 1:1-4	1:5-10	1:11-19	1:20-25	Rev 1:1-3	1:4-6	1:7-11
95	1:12-13	1:14-16	1:17-20	2:1-6	2:7	2:8-9	2:10-11
96	2:12-14	2:15-17	2:18-23	2:24-29	3:1-3	3:4-6	3:7-9
97	3:10-13	3:14-18	3:19-22	4:1-5	4:6-7	4:8-11	5:1-6
98	5:7-14	6:1-8	6:9-17	7:1-8	7:9-17	8:1-6	8:7-12
99	8:13—9:11	9:12-21	10:1-4	10:5-11	11:1-4	11:5-14	11:15-19
100	12:1-4	12:5-9	12:10-18	13:1-10	13:11-18	14:1-5	14:6-12
101	14:13-20	15:1-8	16:1-12	16:13-21	17:1-6	17:7-18	18:1-8
102	18:9—19:4	19:5-10	19:11-16	19:17-21	20:1-6	20:7-10	20:11-15
103	21:1	21:2	21:3-8	21:9-13	21:14-18	21:19-21	21:22-27
104	22:1	22:2	22:3-11	22:12-15	22:16-17	22:18-21	

Week 7 — Day 4 — Today's verses

Eph. 1:17-18 That the God of our Lord Jesus Christ, the Father of glory, may give to you a spirit of wisdom and revelation in the full knowledge of Him, the eyes of your heart having been enlightened, that you may know what is the hope of His calling, and what are the riches of the glory of His inheritance in the saints.

Phil. 3:10-11 To know Him and the power of His resurrection and the fellowship of His sufferings, being conformed to His death, if perhaps I may attain to the out-resurrection from the dead.

Date _____

Week 7 — Day 5 — Today's verses

Phil. 3:5-8 Circumcised the eighth day; of the race of Israel, of the tribe of Benjamin, a Hebrew *born* of Hebrews; as to the law, a Pharisee; as to zeal, persecuting the church; as to the righteousness which is in the law, become blameless. But what things were gains to me, these I have counted as loss on account of Christ. But moreover I also count all things to be loss on account of the excellency of the knowledge of Christ Jesus my Lord, on account of whom I have suffered the loss of all things and count *them* as refuse that I may gain Christ.

Date _____

Week 7 — Day 6 — Today's verses

Phil. 3:13 ...One thing I *do*: Forgetting the things which are behind and stretching forward to the things which are before.

1 Cor. 2:1-2 And I, when I came to you, brothers, came not according to excellence of speech or of wisdom, announcing to you the mystery of God. For I did not determine to know anything among you except Jesus Christ, and this One crucified.

Date _____

Week 7 — Day 1 — Today's verses

Phil. 3:12-14 Not that I have already obtained or am already perfected, but I pursue, if even I may lay hold of that for which I also have been laid hold of by Christ Jesus. Brothers, I do not account of myself to have laid hold; but one thing I *do*: Forgetting the things which are behind and stretching forward to the things which are before, I pursue toward the goal for the prize to which God in Christ Jesus has called *me* upward.

Date _____

Week 7 — Day 2 — Today's verses

Phil. 3:8 But moreover I also count all things to be loss on account of the excellency of the knowledge of Christ Jesus my Lord, on account of whom I have suffered the loss of all things and count *them* as refuse that I may gain Christ.

Gal. 1:15-16 But when it pleased God, who set me apart from my mother's womb and called me through His grace, to reveal His Son in me that I might announce Him as the gospel among the Gentiles, immediately I did not confer with flesh and blood.

Date _____

Week 7 — Day 3 — Today's verses

Col. 1:17-19 And He is before all things, and all things cohere in Him; and He is the Head of the Body, the church; He is the beginning, the Firstborn from the dead, that He Himself might have the first place in all things; for in Him all the fullness was pleased to dwell.

Date _____

Week 8 — Day 1

Today's verses

Phil. 3:8 But moreover I also count all things to be loss on account of the excellency of the knowledge of Christ Jesus my Lord, on account of whom I have suffered the loss of all things and count *them* as refuse that I may gain Christ.

10 To know Him and the power of His resurrection and the fellowship of His sufferings, being conformed to His death.

Date

Week 8 — Day 2

Today's verses

Phil. 3:12-14 Not that I have already obtained or am already perfected, but I pursue, if even I may lay hold of that for which I also have been laid hold of by Christ Jesus. Brothers, I do not account of myself to have laid hold; but one thing *I do*: Forgetting the things which are behind and stretching forward to the things which are before, I pursue toward the goal for the prize to which God in Christ Jesus has called *me* upward.

Date

Week 8 — Day 3

Today's verses

1 Cor. 15:45 ...The last Adam *became* a life-giving Spirit.

Rom. 8:11 And if the Spirit of the One who raised Jesus from the dead dwells in you, He who raised Christ Jesus from the dead will also give life to your mortal bodies through His Spirit who indwells you.

Eph. 2:6 And raised *us* up together with *Him*...

2 Cor. 4:16 Therefore we do not lose heart; but though our outer man is decaying, yet our inner *man* is being renewed day by day.

Date

Week 8 — Day 4

Today's verses

Heb. 4:12 For the word of God is living and operative and sharper than any two-edged sword...

1 Cor. 15:10 But by the grace of God I am what I am; and His grace unto me did not turn out to be in vain, but, on the contrary, I labored more abundantly than all of them, yet not I but the grace of God which is with me.

S. S. 2:8 The voice of my beloved! Now he comes, leaping upon the mountains, skipping upon the hills.

14 My dove, in the clefts of the rock, in the covert of the precipice, let me see your countenance, let me hear your voice; for your voice is sweet, and your countenance is lovely.

Date

Week 8 — Day 5

Today's verses

Phil. 3:10 To know Him and the power of His resurrection and the fellowship of His sufferings, being conformed to His death.

Col. 1:24 I now rejoice in my sufferings on your behalf and fill up on my part that which is lacking of the afflictions of Christ in my flesh for His Body, which is the church.

Date

Week 8 — Day 6

Today's verses

John 1:29 The next day he saw Jesus coming to him and said, Behold, the Lamb of God, who takes away the sin of the world!

12:24 Truly, truly, I say to you, Unless the grain of wheat falls into the ground and dies, it abides alone; but if it dies, it bears much fruit.

2 Tim. 2:10 Therefore I endure all things for the sake of the chosen ones, that they themselves also may obtain the salvation which is in Christ Jesus with eternal glory.

Date

Week 9 — Day 4

Today's verses

Phil. 3:11 If perhaps I may attain to the out-resurrection from the dead.

Rev. 20:6 Blessed and holy is he who has part in the first resurrection; over these the second death has no authority, but they will be priests of God and of Christ and will reign with Him for a thousand years.

Heb. 11:35 Women received their dead by resurrection; and others were tortured *to death*, not accepting deliverance, in order that they might obtain a better resurrection.

_____
Date

Week 9 — Day 5

Today's verses

1 Thes. 5:23 And the God of peace Himself sanctify you wholly, and may your spirit and soul and body be preserved complete, without blame, at the coming of our Lord Jesus Christ.

Eph. 2:5-6 Even when we were dead in offenses, made us alive together with Christ (by grace you have been saved) and raised *us* up together with *Him*....

Rom. 8:6 For the mind set on the flesh is death, but the mind set on the spirit is life and peace.

_____
Date

Week 9 — Day 6

Today's verses

John 14:20 In that day you will know that I *am* in My Father, and you in Me, and I in you.

Phil. 1:21 For to me, to live is Christ...

John 11:25 Jesus said to her, I am the resurrection and the life; he who believes into Me, even if he should die, shall live.

_____
Date

Week 9 — Day 1

Today's verses

Phil. 3:10 To know Him and the power of His resurrection and the fellowship of His sufferings, being conformed to His death.

John 6:57 As the living Father has sent Me and I live because of the Father...

10:10-11 ...I have come that they may have life and may have *it* abundantly. I am the good Shepherd; the good Shepherd lays down His life for the sheep.

_____
Date

Week 9 — Day 2

Today's verses

Rom. 6:3-4 Or are you ignorant that all of us who have been baptized into Christ Jesus have been baptized into His death? We have been buried therefore with Him through baptism into His death, in order that just as Christ was raised from the dead through the glory of the Father, so also we might walk in newness of life.

2 Cor. 4:10-11 Always bearing about in the body the putting to death of Jesus that the life of Jesus also may be manifested in our body. For we who are alive are always being delivered unto death for Jesus' sake that the life of Jesus also may be manifested in our mortal flesh.

_____
Date

Week 9 — Day 3

Today's verses

John 12:24-26 Truly, truly, I say to you, Unless the grain of wheat falls into the ground and dies, it abides alone; but if it dies, it bears much fruit. He who loves his soul-life loses it; and he who hates his soul-life in this world shall keep it unto eternal life. If anyone serves Me, let him follow Me; and where I am, there also My servant will be. If anyone serves Me, the Father will honor him.

32 And I, if I be lifted up from the earth, will draw all men to Myself.

_____
Date

Week 10 — Day 4 — Today's verses

Phil. In nothing be anxious, but in everything, by prayer and petition with thanksgiving, let your requests be made known to God; and the peace of God, which surpasses every man's understanding, will guard your hearts and your thoughts in Christ Jesus.
4:6-7

9 The things which you have also learned and received and heard and seen in me, practice these things; and the God of peace will be with you.

John These things I have spoken to you that in
16:33 Me you may have peace. In the world you have affliction, but take courage; I have overcome the world.

_____
Date

Week 10 — Day 5 — Today's verses

Rom. And we know that all things work to-
8:28 gether for good to those who love God, to those who are called according to His purpose.

Matt. Are not two sparrows sold for an as-
10:29 sarion? And not one of them will fall to the earth apart from your Father.

2 Cor. Therefore we do not lose heart; but
4:16-17 though our outer man is decaying, yet our inner man is being renewed day by day. For our momentary lightness of affliction works out for us, more and more surpassingly, an eternal weight of glory.

_____
Date

Week 10 — Day 6 — Today's verses

Phil. Finally, brothers, what things are true,
4:8 what things are dignified, what things are righteous, what things are pure, what things are lovely, what things are well spoken of, if there is any virtue and if any praise, take account of these things.

Gen. And God said, Let Us make man in Our
1:26 image, according to Our likeness; and let them have dominion...

Matt. In the same way, let your light shine
5:16 before men, so that they may see your good works and glorify your Father who is in the heavens.

_____
Date

Week 10 — Day 1 — Today's verses

Phil. Let your forbearance be known to all
4:5-6 men. The Lord is near. In nothing be anxious...

1:21 For to me, to live is Christ...

2:5 Let this mind be in you, which was also in Christ Jesus.

3:8 But moreover I also count all things to be loss on account of the excellency of the knowledge of Christ Jesus my Lord, on account of whom I have suffered the loss of all things and count them as refuse that I may gain Christ.

_____
Date

Week 10 — Day 2 — Today's verses

Phil. Let your forbearance be known to all
4:5 men. The Lord is near.

2 Cor. But I myself, Paul, entreat you through
10:1 the meekness and gentleness of Christ, who (as you say) in person am base among you, but while absent am bold toward you.

2 Chron. Now give me wisdom and knowledge,
1:10 that I may go out and come in before this people...

_____
Date

Week 10 — Day 3 — Today's verses

Phil. For to me, to live is Christ...
1:21

Matt. "Behold, the virgin shall be with child
1:23 and shall bear a son, and they shall call His name Emmanuel" (which is trans-lated, God with us).

Rom. But what does it say? "The word is near
10:8 you, in your mouth and in your heart," that is, the word of the faith which we proclaim.

_____
Date

Week 11 — Day 4

Today's verses

Phil. 4:12-13 ...In everything and in all things I have learned the secret both to be filled and to hunger, both to abound and to lack. I am able to do all things in Him who empowers me.

John 15:4-5 Abide in Me and I in you....I am the vine; you are the branches. He who abides in Me and I in him, he bears much fruit; for apart from Me you can do nothing.

Eph. 3:8 To me, less than the least of all saints, was this grace given to announce to the Gentiles the unsearchable riches of Christ as the gospel.

_____
Date

Week 11 — Day 5

Today's verses

Phil. 4:11-13 ...I have learned, in whatever circumstances I am, to be content....In everything and in all things I have learned the secret....I am able to do all things in Him who empowers me.

3:8-9 ...That I may gain Christ and be found in Him....

_____
Date

Week 11 — Day 6

Today's verses

Phil. 4:8 Finally, brothers, what things are true, what things are dignified, what things are righteous, what things are pure, what things are lovely, what things are well spoken of, if there is any virtue and if any praise, take account of these things.

13 I am able to do all things in Him who empowers me.

Gal. 2:20 I am crucified with Christ; and it is no longer I who live, but it is Christ who lives in me...

4:19 My children, with whom I travail again in birth until Christ is formed in you.

_____
Date

Week 11 — Day 1

Today's verses

Phil. 4:4 Rejoice in the Lord always; again I will say, rejoice.

11-13 Not that I speak according to lack, for I have learned, in whatever circumstances I am, to be content. I know also how to be abased, and I know how to abound; in everything and in all things I have learned the secret both to be filled and to hunger, both to abound and to lack. I am able to do all things in Him who empowers me.

_____
Date

Week 11 — Day 2

Today's verses

Phil. 4:12 I know also how to be abased, and I know how to abound; in everything and in all things I have learned the secret both to be filled and to hunger, both to abound and to lack.

1 Tim. 3:15-16 But if I delay, I write that you may know how one ought to conduct himself in the house of God, which is the church of the living God, the pillar and base of the truth. And confessedly, great is the mystery of godliness: He who was manifested in the flesh, justified in the Spirit, seen by angels, preached among the nations, believed on in the world, taken up in glory.

_____
Date

Week 11 — Day 3

Today's verses

Phil. 4:11-12 Not that I speak according to lack, for I have learned, in whatever circumstances I am, to be content. I know also how to be abased, and I know how to abound; in everything and in all things I have learned the secret both to be filled and to hunger, both to abound and to lack.

_____
Date

Week 12 — Day 1 — Today's verses

Titus 2:12-13 …We should live soberly and righteously and godly in the present age, awaiting the blessed hope, even the appearing of the glory of our great God and Savior, Jesus Christ.

Phil. 3:20 For our commonwealth exists in the heavens, from which also we eagerly await a Savior, the Lord Jesus Christ.

Eph. 2:19 So then you are no longer strangers and sojourners, but you are fellow citizens with the saints and members of the household of God.

Date _____

Week 12 — Day 2 — Today's verses

Phil. 3:21 Who will transfigure the body of our humiliation to be conformed to the body of His glory, according to His operation by which He is able even to subject all things to Himself.

John 3:6 …That which is born of the Spirit is spirit.

Rom. 12:2 …Be transformed by the renewing of the mind.…

1 John 3:2 Beloved, now we are children of God, and it has not yet been manifested what we will be. We know that if He is manifested, we will be like Him because we will see Him even as He is.

Date _____

Week 12 — Day 3 — Today's verses

Rom. 8:23 And not only so, but we ourselves also, who have the firstfruits of the Spirit, even we ourselves groan in ourselves, eagerly awaiting sonship, the redemption of our body.

Eph. 1:13 In whom you also, having heard the word of the truth, the gospel of your salvation, in Him also believing, you were sealed with the Holy Spirit of the promise.

4:30 And do not grieve the Holy Spirit of God, in whom you were sealed unto the day of redemption.

Date _____

Week 12 — Day 4 — Today's verses

2 Cor. 4:17 For our momentary lightness of affliction works out for us, more and more surpassingly, an eternal weight of glory.

1 Pet. 5:10 But the God of all grace, He who has called you into His eternal glory in Christ Jesus, after you have suffered a little while, will Himself perfect, establish, strengthen, *and* ground *you.*

Rom. 8:17-18 And if children, heirs also; on the one hand, heirs of God; on the other, joint heirs with Christ, if indeed we suffer with *Him* that we may also be glorified with *Him.* For I consider that the sufferings of this present time are not worthy to be compared with the coming glory to be revealed upon us.

Date _____

Week 12 — Day 5 — Today's verses

Heb. 2:10-11 For it was fitting for Him, for whom are all things and through whom are all things, in leading many sons into glory, to make the Author of their salvation perfect through sufferings. For both He who sanctifies and those who are being sanctified are all of One, for which cause He is not ashamed to call them brothers.

1 Thes. 5:23 And the God of peace Himself sanctify you wholly, and may your spirit and soul and body be preserved complete, without blame, at the coming of our Lord Jesus Christ.

Date _____

Week 12 — Day 6 — Today's verses

Col. 1:27 To whom God willed to make known what are the riches of the glory of this mystery among the Gentiles, which is Christ in you, the hope of glory.

2 Thes. 1:10 When He comes to be glorified in His saints and to be marveled at in all those who have believed.…

2 Cor. 3:18 But we all with unveiled face, beholding and reflecting like a mirror the glory of the Lord, are being transformed into the same image from glory to glory, even as from the Lord Spirit.

Rev. 21:10-11 And he…showed me the holy city, Jerusalem, coming down out of heaven from God, having the glory of God.…

Date _____